ALL AMERICAN HEARTS

TRUE STORIES OF AMERICA'S WOUNDED WARRIORS

D1605630

JOSEPH BADDICK

Aperture Press

ISBN 978-0-9889351-5-0
Library of Congress Control Number: 2013939021

First Edition, June 2013

Cover and interior designed by Stephen Wagner.

This book is dedicated to
America's Wounded Warriors

For Chris & Michelle,
an inspirational book
for the rough times.
All the best – Joe

Joseph Baddick

CONTENTS

Acknowledgements   7

Introduction
    by LtCol Oliver L. North, USMC (Ret.)   9

Foreword   11

The Purple Heart   13

1. There's No Such Thing As A Bad Day   21

2. Everything Went To Shit   29

3. The Humvee Looked Like Swiss Cheese   39

4. Alright, I Wanna Live, I Wanna Live   43

5. I Never Knew Skin Could Hang Off
     A Body Like That   53

6. He Looked Like Darth Vader   59

7. I Went To War And Garrison Broke Out   67

8. Hey Doc, I Think I Need A Band-Aid   71

9. Unless The Kid Has Cable TV, I Don't
     Think It's A Real Grave   77

10. May, Injured In May   83

11. Oh No, Not Again   87

12. Ya Gotta Stop Sarge, Really   105

13. Zhari District, Kandahar Province   111

14. You're The Best Damn Squad Leader
     I Ever Had   115

15. I'm Not Losing Another One   129

16. It's A Marlboro, Thank God   135

17. Willie And Me   153

18. I'd Like To Get Out And Play
   Some Golf   165
19. Persistence   171
20. I Was Covered In Sparkles   181
21. Blood Wings   185

Afterword   195
Photographs   197
About the Author   205

ACKNOWLEDGMENTS

I would like to thank Walter Reed National Military Medical Center in Bethesda, Maryland for taking such good care of our Wounded Warriors and allowing me to tell their stories. The staff was, at all times, courteous and helpful.

Thanks to all the military liaisons who assisted me when I needed information, dates, and times for interviews.

I would like to thank Ft. Bragg for being a home to me and my son, A.J. Baddick, when we were in the service. I would like to thank the Command Staff for turning out such fine young men and women and carrying on the tradition of 'America's Guard of Honor.'

I would like to thank Ms. Rita Cosby for assisting me with a very special part of this book.

I would like to thank The Purple Heart Hall of Honor in Windsor, New York, and Mr. Pete Bedrossian, program director, for his assistance.

Thanks to Sharon Wells Wagner and her son, Steve Wagner, my publishers.

INTRODUCTION

by LtCol Oliver L. North, USMC (Ret.)

I first met Joe Baddick a few years ago at a Freedom Concert with Sean Hannity in Jackson, New Jersey. Joe handed me a book titled *My Hero My Son.* The cover revealed a vivid Gold Star Pin and I immediately knew this man had lost his son in combat. Joe told me how young "A.J." died in Iraq saving the life of one soldier and attempting to rescue another, when his unit was called up to ambush insurgents near Abu Ghraib prison in September of 2003. Joe was immensely proud of A.J., who had followed in his father's footsteps. Both had served proudly with the 82nd Airborne's 504th Parachute Infantry Regiment. With a great deal of courage and a tremor in his voice, Joe described his son's heroism.

Over the course of the next several years, *My Hero My Son* inspired many readers to reach out to Joe. Letters and emails poured in. Among them were Gold Star widows, mothers, and fathers like Joe. Some were young men and women who'd been wounded in Iraq and Afghanistan, some who had served with A.J. Others were civilians who realized for the first time that serving one's country was truly a sacrifice. Joe answered every letter, email, and phone call, and in so doing, discovered his work was not yet finished. Thus began his odyssey to tell the stories of others who had served.

All American Hearts, Joe's new book, tells the true stories of America's Wounded Warriors, brave men and women of our armed forces who are recipients of the Purple Heart Medal. Over the course of a year and a half, Joe made frequent trips to

Walter Reed National Military Medical Center at Bethesda to interview military personnel wounded in Iraq and Afghanistan. Each unique account is woven into an intricate tapestry of tragedy, suffering, courage, and determination. The result is a compelling collection of true stories guaranteed to educate and inspire the reader.

As the recipient of two Purple Hearts, I have a great deal of empathy for these young warriors. They instill in us a sense of pride and have taught us the true meaning of service. Service is selfless. It is borne of courage and love for one's country. They truly are America's heroes.

LtCol Oliver L. North, USMC (Ret.) is the author of the American Heroes book series and the co-founder of Freedom Alliance, an organization that provides college scholarships to the children of U.S. military personnel killed or permanently disabled in the line of duty.

FOREWORD

All American Hearts is a compilation of stories from Purple Heart recipients in their own words. It covers the wars in Iraq and Afghanistan. These personal stories will take you to the battlefields where our brave warriors are fighting right now.

I have a place in my own heart for our brave men and women who have volunteered to go into harm's way to do their duty for the United States of America. I served with the 82nd Airborne Division and my son, Sgt. A.J. Baddick, gave his life serving with the 82nd Airborne's 504th Parachute Infantry Regiment in Iraq.

I have made numerous trips to Walter Reed National Military Medical Center in Bethesda, Maryland to visit and interview our Wounded Warriors. I have also met wounded soldiers on my many visits to Ft. Bragg, North Carolina. These men and women are some of our country's best and brightest. I thank them for all they do to keep our country safe and our freedom intact. It is an honor for me to tell their stories.

THE PURPLE HEART

W hat is the Purple Heart? It is the military decoration awarded in the name of the President of the United States to those who have been wounded or killed in combat while serving with the United States military on or after April 5, 1917. The precursor to this medal was the Badge of Military Merit, which was made from purple cloth in the shape of a heart and edged in silver braid. It was intended to be worn over the left breast of the military uniform.

The Purple Heart's roots lie deep within our nation's history. The United States' first military decoration was the Fidelity Medallion, which was issued only once, by the Continental Congress in 1870, to three soldiers who aided in the capture of British Army Major John Andre. Having assisted the traitor Benedict Arnold, Andre was convicted of treason and hanged. The Fidelity Medallion, which bore a silver heart and the words "Amor Patriae Vincit" ("The love of country conquers") was awarded to Andre's three captors for their specific actions. It was then retired. For this reason, the medallion is usually considered the first—but not the oldest—United States military decoration. That distinction lies with an award that was created just two years later.

During the American Revolution, General George Washington wished to reward meritorious acts among his enlisted men; however, the Continental Congress forbade him from granting promotions in rank for such a purpose. He instead created the Badge of Military Merit. On August 7, 1782, as the end of the war drew near, Washington gave the following decree: "The General, ever desirous to cherish a virtuous ambition in his soldiers, as well as to foster and encourage every species of military merit, directs that whenever any singularly meritorious action is performed, the author of it shall be permitted to wear on his facings, over his left breast, the figure of a heart in purple cloth, edged with a narrow lacing or binding. Not only instances of unusual gallantry, but also of extraordinary fidelity and essential service in any way shall meet with due reward."

The first Badge of Military Merit was awarded to twenty-six-year-old Sergeant Elijah Churchill of Enfield, Connecticut, a member of the Fourth Troop of the Second Continental Dragoons. In 1780 and 1781 Sergeant Churchill participated in two daring raids against British outposts, his actions resulting in the weakening of enemy forces. General Washington said of him: "He acted in a very conspicuous and singularly meritorious part; that at the head of the attack, he not only acquitted himself with great gallantry, firmness, and address; but that the surprise, in one instance, and the success of the attack in the other, proceeded in a considerable degree from his conduct and management... Now therefore Know Ye, that the aforesaid Sergeant Elijah Churchill, hath faithfully and truly deserved, and has been properly invested with the Honorary Badge of Military Merit, and is authorized to pass and repass all guards and military posts as fully and amply as any Commissioned Officer whatever, and is hereby recommended to that favorable notice which a Brave and

Faithful Soldier deserves from his countrymen."

After the American Revolution, the Badge of Military Merit fell out of use and was not proposed again until after World War I. On October 10, 1927, Army Chief of Staff General Charles Summerall directed that a bill be sent to Congress, "to revive the Badge of Military Merit." The bill was withdrawn and no action was ever taken.

In 1931 General Douglas MacArthur revisited the case and began work on a new design for the Badge of Military Merit. He employed the Washington Commission of Fine Arts. It was decided that models for the new medal would be submitted by three sculptors. John R. Sinnock, who worked for the Philadelphia Mint, presented the winning design.

In a fitting gesture, the Purple Heart medal was reborn on February 22, 1932—George Washington's two-hundredth birthday.

The medal's design is elegant and historically symbolic. Its focal point is a gold portrait of George Washington in profile, set within a purple heart-shaped field. A gold border surrounds the medal's core, at the top of which lies President Washington's coat of arms—a white shield with red bars and stripes flanked by green leaves. Written on the medal's reverse side are three words: *FOR MILITARY MERIT*. A purple ribbon with white stripes completes the design.

Approximately 500,000 Purple Heart medals were manufactured during World War II prior to the invasion of Japan, in anticipation of the large number of casualties that military planners expected. It was believed that the Japanese forces would fight to the last man in defense of their homeland. Fortunately, the invasion never took place because President Harry Truman decided to drop atomic bombs on Japan. The Japanese capitulated, bringing an end to the Pacific war and saving countless lives.

In all the years since World War II ended, this supply of Purple Heart medals has not been exhausted. Approximately 100,000 medals still remain. Because there are so many left, it is possible to have them on-site in the Middle East theatre of operations to award to soldiers as they are wounded.

In 1952, President Harry Truman made the medal retroactive back to World War I. There is no accurate way of knowing how many Purple Heart medals have been given out over the years. The following numbers are approximations gathered from different sources:

World War I	...	240,000
World War II	...	1,070,000
Korean War	...	136,800
Vietnam War	...	350,700
Persian Gulf War	...	615
Afghanistan War	...	18,900 (as of June 5, 2010)
Iraq War	...	35,365 (as of June 5, 2010)

The Purple Heart medal is awarded to any member of the United States armed forces or U.S. civilian who, while serving with the military, has been wounded, killed, or has died after being wounded. It is awarded in the name of the President of the United States. Though low in order of precedence on the Pyramid of Honor, the Purple Heart is one of the most highly recognized and respected medals. It cannot be earned through courage, exceptional service, or achievement. It signifies only one thing: sacrifice. It represents the blood that has been shed in defense of liberty and freedom. This is where it differs from all other military decorations.

Notable recipients of the Purple Heart Award include: Staff Sergeant Salvatore Giunta, the first living person since the Vietnam War to receive the Medal of Honor; John F. Kennedy; General Colin Powell; John McCain; Lt. Colonel Oliver North; General Wesley Clark; General Eric Shinseki; Band of Brothers member Major Dick Winters; actors Audie Murphy, Charles Durning, Lee Marvin, Charles Bronson, James Arness, and James Garner; writers Rod Serling, Kurt Vonnegut Jr., Ron Kovic, Charles Franklin Hildebrand, and James Jones; athletes Pat Tillman, Rocky Bleier, and Warren Spahn; and film director Oliver Stone.

As the time of writing, it is estimated that 1.7 million Purple Hearts have been awarded.

Badge of Military Merit

Fidelity Medallion

ALL AMERICAN HEARTS

1

THERE'S NO SUCH THING AS A BAD DAY

My name is Jonathan Tompkins. I was born in 1982 in Quakertown, Pennsylvania and I grew up in East Greenville, Pennsylvania. I spent some time in Florida and a year in Connecticut before joining the Marine Corps in February, 2000.

I enlisted in the Marine Corps because I had an older brother in the Navy and two older brothers in the Marine Corps. I looked up to all of them, so I thought it was appropriate that I do the same. I thought joining the military would make me a better, more responsible person and give me leadership qualities that would benefit me as I got older.

On February 26, 2000 I left for Parris Island, South Carolina for my basic training. After three months, I returned home for ten days leave then headed off to Marine Combat Training at Camp Lejeune, North Carolina. Upon completion of that course, I was sent to Twenty-Nine Palms, California for my MOS (Military Occupational Specialty) schooling as a field radio operator.

In July of 2006 we were sent to Camp Pendleton, California to begin our training for deployment. After two and a half months of pre-deployment work up, we left for Kuwait. We spent one week there in transition before heading into Iraq. Our base was located at Al-Asad Airbase, Al-Asad, Iraq.

The date was 4 April. Our mission that day was to run TCNs (third country nationals) from Al-Asad to Al-Najaf. The mission was to act as convoy security for the Iraqi Army as they relocated to a new base. Once they were dropped off, we headed north to Camp Fallujah to spend the night. The next morning, 5 April, we had our ten vehicles heading back to our base at Al-Asad to maintain and prepare our vehicles for the next mission. For this mission, my vehicle was moved from the scout element to second to last vehicle in the convoy. I thought this was extremely unusual.

On our way from Camp Fallujah to Al-Asad our convoy entered a marketplace in Sacagawea, just north of the middle of the city. The lead vehicle pointed out a possible IED (improvised explosive device) on the right hand side of the road. The device looked like a muffler with copper wire coming out of it, running off into the desert. We had a problem. The suspected IED had split our convoy in two, causing a possibly dangerous situation for the entire convoy. We stopped approximately three hundred meters short of the IED, and the vehicle in front of us pushed up three hundred meters past the IED, separating us by six hundred meters. I radioed for the convoy to halt.

On this particular day, my vehicle was one Marine short. That left us with a gunner, me, and the driver. Here was the problem. The gunner and driver were unable to leave the vehicle in case of an attack. Because of logistics, I exited the vehicle to verify whether this was indeed a real IED. I dismounted the truck, walked slowly toward the IED, using my rifle scope to assess the situation. When I got to within five to ten meters I could clearly see the suspected IED with the copper wires was a hoax. I realized it was put there to get me out of my vehicle.

I thought about the training I had regarding such situations and tried to remain calm, showing restraint. I looked at my gunner, saw him in the turret, and I used arm signals to indicate caution. I made my way slowly back to the vehicle, pausing here and there to act as if I didn't know what was going on. I was thinking that this was a hoax, a ploy for an ambush, a way for the insurgents to get more Marines out of their trucks. Once I returned to the vehicle, I turned to my gunner and said, "Something's not right; I have a bad gut feeling." After taking one last look around, I reached for the door handle and felt a shock. It felt like an electric shock. I yelled out, "That hurt." When I tried to breathe, I couldn't. I suddenly felt a stabbing, stinging pain in my chest. I put my hand under my armpit to feel what happened. I moved my hand around and when I looked, it was covered in blood. I was shot by a sniper that was in a car in the marketplace.

I knew at that point, I needed to inform the others in the convoy. It was my job to call for a medevac and my training took over. Our training teaches us self-aid. I tried to perform this on myself and I was also calling for MP2, the call sign for our platoon commander. My response was, "MP2, MP2, this is ghost one. I'm hit, I'm hit. Sniper, right hand side, approximately 1,000 to 1,500 meters out."

The response back was, "How bad?"

I responded, "Wait one."

While I was assessing the situation, the platoon commander said to take immediate action to counter the attack. At that point, every other vehicle turned their weapons to the east side, laying down a base of fire. Suddenly, another IED was detonated. We started receiving small arms fire from the right side. The gunners laid down a base of fire so the helicopter would be able to land and medevac me off the road. As I opened up my protective vest, all I remember is blood spraying out of my chest, all over the inside of the truck. I got back on the radio and said, "MP2, MP2, I'm bleeding out." Then, "I need urgent surgical medevac." At that same time the closest corpsman was in the vehicle on the other side of the IED. All I remember was looking out the window, seeing corpsman Doc Ferrer jump out of vehicle MP6, grabbing his med bag and running past the IED towards me. I radioed to the Doc to return to his vehicle so he wouldn't get himself shot.

With total disregard for his own safety, he continued towards my vehicle. Doc Ferrer pulled me out of the truck, leaned me up against it, and immediately started treating me. At this time, we were still under fire and I had a bad feeling about our situation. I pulled out my pistol, as it was the only weapon within my reach. I began firing in the direction of the small arms fire. I paused, and with only a few rounds left, I returned to my radio, asking the vehicle behind us to pull up on the other side, to sandwich us in. As soon as the other vehicle pulled up next to us, they received a sniper's bullet through the passenger side window, which was meant for Doc, but went right through me. I turned to Doc Ferrer, asking for morphine, but I was bleeding out too badly. The morphine would cause my blood to thin, making me bleed even more. Doc turned to me and told me he was going to perform something that was going to hurt really bad. He pulled out his knife, inserted it into the middle of my ribcage, slicing me open from my lower rib to my armpit. He then proceeded to stick his hand inside my chest cavity, pulling fragmented and shattered ribs from my lung. While holding the ribs back, he pulled my chest muscles out and wrapped them around my rib, preventing them from puncturing my lung so I could breathe.

As he did this, I told Corporal Rodriguez, "Tell my family I love them."

He stopped me and said, "You're gonna make it out alive; you'll be fine." He held my hand as the Doc worked on me. I looked at him and asked if I would really make it out alive. He looked at me and said, "What do you want me to tell your family if you don't?"

I told him, in such a short time, everything about me, my family, and my deepest thoughts. After that, he cried. In an instant, I took my pistol and turned it on myself. The thought in my head was, I would rather take my own life rather than let some coward determine my fate. As I raised the pistol, the trigger was halfway in. As soon as it touched my temple, Rodriguez jumped up from where he was and snatched the pistol from my hand. At that point, I yelled orders for him to return my pistol to me. He looked at me, stunned, and he said that this was an unlawful order and he wouldn't follow it. While Doc Ferrer and Corporal Rodriguez were trying to save me, our convoy was still under small arms fire.

The last thing I remember was the medevac helicopter landing and seeing the stretcher being pulled out for me. They laid me down on the stretcher, causing the blood to suddenly flood my lungs. They sat me up so I could breath, but it was too late. I had flat-lined. I was told later that as soon as I was loaded on the helicopter, my heart started, but I went into a coma. I was flown to Camp Fallujah for a few hours but because they lacked the medical care that I needed, I was transferred to Al-Asad's trauma center which had recently been completed and had opened an intensive care unit.

After flat-lining a few more times, I was flown to Ramstein Air Base in Germany where I spent three days in a medically-induced coma. On the night of April 9th, I was flown to National Naval Medical Center in Bethesda, Maryland where I spent another three weeks in a coma. While at NNMC, I had my organs packaged in order to prevent contamination. My time at NNMC included forty plus surgeries, including removal of my gall bladder, seventy percent of my liver, a large part of my intestines, part of my stomach, and my ribs were replaced with medical material to replace my original ribs.

My surgical scar begins at my belt line and continues to my sternum, along with smaller surgical scars on my torso. The hospital stay was a total of seven months, but the first five months were mostly surgical complications. My body had a very difficult time adjusting, making it hard for my rehab to begin. The medical teams at NNMC had the chance to introduce new medical procedures since nothing else was working, and, considering my case and injuries, they were able to use the new procedures in hopes of finding new and improved methods that would soon help others injured as well.

After my incident, the other Marines returned to base to drop off our supplies. Everyone else from the convoy returned to base safely. After speaking to other Marines that were there, I was told I was taken to Al-Taqaddum Air Base, west of Fallujah, before they flew me to Al-Asad. The Marines set up a fire watch every four to eight hours to monitor my status.

The last two months of my hospital stay was learning how to walk again and reintroducing use of my fine motor skills. Those two months were the most tedious. I received my Purple Heart in June of 2008 at National Naval Medical Center by Commandant of the Marine Corps, General James T. Conway and Sergeant Major of the Marine Corps, Carlton Kent.

I spent eleven years in the Marine Corps and I am currently retired and returning to college for Business Management. I hope to graduate in 2013 and continue on to my MBA while looking into starting my own business. I reside in Macungie, Pennsylvania. Since my incident, I and two other individuals have started a non-profit organization called Keystone Wounded Warriors. Our mission is to honor the daily sacrifices made by our servicemen and women who were wounded on or after September 11, 2001. We focus on the financial, physical, mental and professional development of transitioning back into civilian life. You can check out our website at: www.

keystonewarriors.com.

My long term goals are to own a business or have a job that provides a secure lifestyle for my family. I see myself moving into a big city and choosing the hardest path possible because I always like a challenge, and when I do find one, I never back away.

There is no such thing as a bad day. Everything happens for a reason, and my reasons for being here are now becoming clear. I have realized that the harder the challenge, the greater the reward. I don't let the small, minute things bother me because it's those things that can hinder one's true path.

2

EVERYTHING WENT TO SHIT

My name is Idi Mallari. I was born and raised in the port of Veracruz, Mexico. At the age of fourteen, I came to the United States and moved to Chicago, Illinois along with my family, seeking the American dream. Arriving in the United States, speaking merely a few sentences of English, I started the journey towards my dream.

I graduated from Morton East High School, class of 2004. However, my academic career took a pause after high school when I left for Army Combat Basic Training.

After 9/11, I felt the urge to answer the call of duty for the country that opened its doors to my family and me. While my classmates applied for college, I enlisted in the United States Army for four years as a Combat Medic. Upon graduating from high school, I reported to basic training where my commitment to the United States military began. During my four-year journey, I served and deployed with the 82nd Airborne Division's 505th Parachute Infantry Regiment stationed at Fort Bragg, North Carolina. During that time, I was called upon to be a Team Leader, Squad Leader, Section Leader, Platoon Sergeant, Infantry Platoon Medic, Infantry Company Medic, and Advanced Life Support Team member in Iraq.

My military awards include the Combat Medical Badge, Army Parachutist Badge, Air Assault Badge, Army Meritorious Unit Commendation, the Purple Heart, Army Commendation Medal with Valor Device, Army Achievement Medal, Good Conduct Medal, National Defense Medal, Iraqi Campaign Medal, Humanitarian Service Medal, Noncommissioned Officer Professional Development Ribbon, Army Service Ribbon, and Overseas Service Ribbon.

The following is from my diary as I remembered it in April of 2007 in Iraq:

19 April 2007: I do not remember what happened today. Today was a normal day in the sandbox. I expect another regular day tomorrow.

20 April 2007: The snipers and I just received our next mission. The mission is to conduct a seventy-two-hour watch position on a Canal Route.

SP (start point) time is 0030 hours. A 1st Cav Bradley will be dropping us off by the Iraqi Police Station. We will then move by foot to our first position. It sounds like a regular mission. I am packing three meals (tuna), and three 1-liter bottles of water, a meal and a bottle of water per day. I can't afford to carry more than that. My aid bag is very heavy already. I'm packing my poncho liner, two pairs of socks, and enough candy to chew to help keep me awake at night while on security. The next seventy-two hours do not sound very exciting. Charlie X-ray. Out.

21 April 2007: The snipers and I departed our patrol base

in As Sadah at 0030 hours. We mounted a 1st Cav Bradley and then dismounted at the Iraqi Police Station. We began our movement to the position along the Canal Route. We moved through the palm grove located on the outskirts of the town. We moved tactically, as expected from the sniper squad. All the locals were in the houses enjoying their naps. We crossed several canals then started moving rapidly until we were faced with a wide canal. We had no choice but to maneuver around a house which was located along the canal.

The snipers and I carefully maneuvered, but the house dog started barking. The owners woke up. We needed to get out of there fast. We moved rapidly, but as we moved, we started to sink. The ground was very wet due to the canal. The smell was horrible. The owners had a cow which slept along the fence we were maneuvering around. My steps kept getting deeper in the soggy ground. Finally, I sank deeper into the soggy, smelly ground, which happened to be where the cow shit. An occupant of the house, a kid, came out to see why the dog was barking. I stood up and pointed my weapon at the kid. The snipers and I moved out of there as fast as we could. It was almost sunrise and we were not at our position yet. After walking a couple hundred meters, we found a good hide site. Around 0600 hours the locals started working in their fields. We carefully watched them go about their jobs. Our position was then compromised as the locals climbed the palm trees and watched us from above.

I have cow shit all over my uniform. I will change my socks as soon as I can. This is just the beginning of a seventy-two hour mission. Life sucks. This is definitely a "Fuck My Life" moment. Charlie X-ray. Out.

21 April 2007: (approximately 2200 hours) Our hiding position was compromised early in the morning as the locals worked their fields. We are moving to a new hide site along the Canal Route. We will be moving cautiously to our new hide site. It has been a peaceful day overall. So far, it has been a regular mission. Only fifty-one hours to go. Charlie X-ray. Out.

22 April 2007: We received new orders. Collapse present position and return to patrol base at the end of night. A Bradley will pick us up and return us to As Sadah. Charlie X-ray. Out.

23 April 2007: We got picked up last night. When we got back I saw a familiar face. It was Cain. The "Workhorse" (5-73rd Cavalry Bravo Troop, 2nd Platoon) were in As Sadah. I don't know their medic.

I found out who the medic for the Workhorse was. He was PFC Knoll. I had met him before in Caldwell when he just arrived at the unit. He was like any new guy in the Army who was just informed he was going to deploy. His story was very similar to Doc Gilbert. Gilbert got to 3-505 and was given a rifle and was put on the next flight to Iraq in his first deployment. PFC Knoll was in Gilbert's shoes this time. The plan for today is to inspect PFC Knoll's aid bag and test his skills. Charlie-X-ray. Out.

A peaceful day just turned into the shittiest and worst day of my life.

There was chaos everywhere. You only see things like this in the movies. I never thought that I would ever be a part of something like this. Just minutes ago, two car bombs exploded just outside our patrol base.

I heard shots earlier and I disregarded them. It just sounded like any other day. Corporal Rudy and I had taken a picture because he was heading to Alpha Troop to be their senior medic at anytime. He packed and left all his gear outside the aid station. We disregarded the sounds of bullets. Then, out of nowhere, I was thrown from one side of the aid station to the other side. Dust and dirt were everywhere. I could not see in front of me due to the dirt and dust. It was like one of those moments when everything goes to shit. This was one of those moments. I got up and Corporal Rudy ran outside for his equipment. Then again, just seconds after the first blast, I was thrown to the other side of the aid station. Medical equipment was flying in all directions. More dirt and dust. My first thought then was where Corporal Rudy was. I called up his name, but there was no answer. I thought he was gone, but in the cloud of dirt and dust, he reached for my hand. He was alive. Rudy was alive.

I put my body armor on as people came into the now destroyed aid station. I heard screams and calls for medics. Rudy and I grabbed our aid bags and with the sounds of bullets everywhere, we started looking for people. It was difficult because of all the dirt and dust made it almost impossible to see what was ahead. Then finally, I came upon someone down. It was Marshall, and there were other soldiers with him. He was the FO (forward observer) for Workhorse.

It was an image I was not expecting. We took him inside our now destroyed aid station and started treating him. Marshall's arm was gone and I immediately went to work stopping the bleeding. I then left Spear with Marshall as I went out to look for more casualties.

Everyone was a casualty, but Rudy and I only treated the worst ones. Corporal Rudy was working on Gonzalez. Outside, the Workhorse platoon sergeant, Sergeant First Class Lillie, came over to me and said, "Mallari, I am missing many guys and my platoon leader. I asked where he last saw them and pointed to a wall which, just this morning had been a two-floor wing of our patrol base. This was now gone. I wasn't sure how to react, but started digging with my hands through the debris only to find nothing. There was more debris in front of me and exposed beams that had supported this building.

In a second, my life flashed in front of me.

I then asked where Knoll was because he needed to be in the aid station helping. SFC Lillie responded simply with, "I'm missing Knoll."

Then I remembered the last time I saw him. It was this morning when I inspected his aid bag and equipment. His stuff was in perfect order.

Doc Adams, Bravo Troop senior medic, had already taken care of Adams, just as he did when I was one of his medics. I then had Knoll perform the skills test. He did an IV stick and did it well, not missing his target. His bleeding and airway test was right on. Doc Adams had taught him well. I was impressed. Knoll was also disciplined and respectful. When we were done, he headed out for a patrol with his platoon. The Workhorse was my first platoon. I knew everyone, except the new guys.

After training, I stopped by the room they were staying in to say hi. Almost everyone was there. I talked to them for a while, reminiscing about the days when I was their medic. They made fun of me because of how I always did body checks after training. We laughed a lot and I wished I could have stayed longer with them. On my way to the aid station, I saw Lt. Gasper. I spoke to him and said, "Sir, I like your medic, Knoll, and I might bring him to my company."

He replied, "No Doc, you guys keep taking our medics, not this time though. I'm sorry." I was glad he felt that way; it only meant that he liked Knoll. I went back to the clinic and that was the last time I saw them. Knoll returned from his patrol and we did some more training. Then I told him to get some rest before his next patrol. He went and joined Workhorse in their room. Twenty minutes later everything went to shit, and I was on the ground after being thrown from one side of the building to the other.

Someone then said, "Doc, they need you at the aid station."

I had now come back to reality and went back to continue working on Marshall with Spear. Medevac was on its way. The sounds of bullets in the background, the dirt and dust, the blood, and people yelling and screaming made everything at this moment seem unreal. I watched the media coverage of 9/11 six years earlier and this was it. A 9/11 in As Sadah. It was unreal.

The Medevac was on the ground. Doc Rudy and I had already packed everything for medevac and we took everyone to the Blackhawk helicopter. Our HLZ (helicopter landing zone), was 100 meters from us and, in the dust and confusion, we carried everyone for evac, while flying bullets hit the first thing in their path. Everyone was loaded, and when I turned around there were walking wounded approaching the Blackhawk.

By this time, support had arrived. Alpha troop was here and the sounds of bullets had ceased. M1 Abrams Tanks and Bradleys now occupied the streets. On my way back from the Helicopter Landing Zone, I saw Major Rather and I could not hold it together anymore; I broke down into tears. The report was that there were eight people missing and they were all from Workhorse. The patrol base was reduced to half its size. Soldiers from different units were arriving now. Life, as I knew it, was over in seconds. Major Rather reassured me and said everything would be okay. The worst of my life was not over yet. Eight soldiers from Workhorse were still missing. No one stopped digging through the dirt and debris until we found them. As we pulled everyone out, the medics did everything they could to bring them back. And as night fell, no one stopped working until our brothers in arms were recovered. IVs were given to many who had been working all day under the blazing sun. Not one soldier stopped or complained until we had 100% accountability.

The official report showed that two SVBIEDs (suicide vehicle borne improvised explosive device) drove through the road barriers set up around the perimeter and exploded, collapsing the north side of a two-story building. I was located twenty meters away from the blast at the north end of the patrol base, one room away from the collapsed building.

I sustained a concussion and abrasions to the left side of my head, and contusions from the two blasts. I continued to assess casualties by providing medical attention and assisting in securing the patrol base. I was presented with my Purple Heart by Colonel David Sutherland, Brigade Commander of 1st Cavalry, 5-73rd.

RIP (rest in peace) to the nine Workhorse men who were lost on 23 April 2007. You have not been forgotten. We will meet at the final manifest. Charlie X-ray. Out.

At the end of my fifteen month deployment in Iraq, I decided to remain in the Army and pursue a career as an Army Officer at the United States Military Academy. Transitioning from soldier to scholar was challenging; but, I managed to meet the demands of West Point.

My physics professor, Lieutenant Colonel Kraig Sheetz, inspired me to pursue a career in Nuclear Engineering. I am interested in researching advanced, safe and renewable sources of alternative energy as fossil fuel becomes more limited. I hope to apply this research in the Army, and plan to carry these new ideas over to the civilian sector, allowing society, as a whole, to benefit and grow.

In my personal time, I volunteer at West Point and in the surrounding community to help those in need by distributing meals during the holidays, donating blood and platelets, mentoring high school students in underprivileged areas, explaining that a person with humble beginnings can grow and achieve great things.

Additionally, I participate in a leadership forum in the

Academy to discuss leadership topics with young leaders in high school. I am also a member of the West Point Spanish Club, with one of its missions being to promote cultural cohesion, awareness, and information about what educational opportunities are available to minorities outside of West Point. I am aspiring to be a leader/scholar of character and be an example that represents excellence through hard work, dedication, and commitment.

I graduated from West Point on 26 May, 2012.

3

THE HUMVEE LOOKED
LIKE SWISS CHEESE

My name is Kelly Oldfather and I'm from El Granada, California.

I joined the military in April 1988, mainly to get some direction in my life and to experience some adventure.

My basic training was at Fort Jackson, South Carolina and my advanced training was at Fort Gordon, Georgia. I have been in the military for approximately fifteen years.

I was involved in the Gulf War first, deploying from Germany while serving on active duty. I deployed two more times after that; once to Iraq in 2004 and then to Afghanistan in 2006.

On the day I received my wounds, I drove my Humvee over an IED (Improvised Explosive Device). My mission was to drive my commander from Baghdad to Baqouba and then back to Tikrit after a commander's conference in Baghdad.

The mission began normally as we convoyed from Tikrit to Baqouba to pick up another officer for the conference. We then headed to Baghdad and picked up supplies for our company and headed back to Tikrit.

The unit I served with was the 324th Psychological

Operations Company out of Aurora, Colorado. The job I held while in Iraq was as a Psyop (Psychological Operations) Sergeant, a 37 Fox. However, on the day I was wounded, I was just a driver for my commander. In my vehicle, besides me, were the commander, my gunner, and our Iraqi interpreter who held dual citizenship. We also had three other vehicles with us for convoy purposes. I was driving on a main highway between Baghdad and Baqouba when the incident occurred where I got wounded. I drove over a buried IED that turned out to be a mortar round. The explosion from the mortar round tore through the engine block of the Humvee and into the main passenger compartment of the vehicle. After it was all over, the Humvee looked like Swiss cheese.

I ended up having a blown out eardrum in my left ear. I received shrapnel in my right arm and some shrapnel fragments in both my legs. We had to recover ourselves from the IED blast, due to the fact that we could not raise anyone on the radios for help. Once we got back to camp at Baqouba we were able to get medical attention. I remained in Iraq and recovered from my wounds there.

At the present time, I live in Oro Valley, Arizona and I'm attending school. I'm working on a Bachelor of Science degree in natural resources. I am also still serving in the military. I just recently re-enlisted in the Arizona National Guard.

My long term goal is to just enjoy life and finish out my Army career.

I believe I was given a second chance that day for a reason. I would do it all again. I remember that day as if it were yesterday, and it doesn't really bother me at all. I'm proud that I'm able to serve my country. Besides, if I hadn't gone to Iraq, I wouldn't have met my husband. My future husband was the driver of the vehicle behind me in the convoy when the IED went off that day.

4

ALRIGHT, I WANNA LIVE,
I WANNA LIVE

My name is Zachary Albert Pagano; my fellow soldiers call me Zap.

I am originally from Charlottesville, Virginia, but professionally I'm from Fort Bragg, North Carolina. I signed an ROTC contract in 2006. My mom didn't want me to join the Army at all, but I think she would have disowned me if I had enlisted right after high school which was my initial plan. However, my recruiter told me he thought I was officer material. I'm not sure if that was a compliment or not. I was commissioned a Lieutenant in December of 2009.

My family has had quite a few guys get killed in various wars. I think I'm actually the first person to survive a war and receive a Purple Heart.

My mother's cousin Joe was a Navy pilot, shot down over Viet Nam. My family was told by the Navy for over thirty years that he had died.

Actually, a few years ago my family found out, thanks to research at The Joint Mia/Pow Accounting Command, that he had survived. They found the remains of his co-pilot and from there were able to ascertain that he had been captured, tortured, and died there.

Then there was my mother's uncle Roger who was a Major in the Marine Corps and fought on Saipan in WWII. He died from the wounds he received on Saipan about six months later. He was awarded the Navy Cross. Then on my father's side, he had eleven uncles in WWII, most of them in the actual shooting war. One was a BAR (Browning Automatic Rifle) gunner. Another was assigned to blow up bunkers and obstacles. They were at Omaha Beach in Normandy.

I attended the Leadership, Development and Assessment Course at Fort Lewis, Washington. Basically, I joined the Army because I wanted to command and be a part of my generation's war. I wanted to be able to look back and say, "I was a part of it."

My first deployment was in February of 2012 as a 1st Lieutenant with the 508th Parachute Infantry Regiment, 82nd Airborne Division out of Fort Bragg, North Carolina. We were assigned to the Zhari District, Kandahar Province, Afghanistan. This was a very complex and interesting environment made up of mostly Pashtuns with deep ties to Mullah Omar. It was a key area with many powerful people.

Around our AO (Area of Operations), outside of the main town of Senjary, was very lush vegetation consisting of mulberry trees and pomegranate trees, along with poppy fields and grape vines growing on walls along the perimeter. There were also canals running along the fields for irrigation. The town of Senjary itself is a mixture of mud and brick buildings with very narrow alleyways. It's a virtual maize. We had more checkpoints going in and out of Senjary than the rest of the battalion. The checkpoints were manned by the ALP (Afghan Local Police) and ANA (Afghan National Army).

Our FOB (Forward Operations Base) was a twenty minute drive west of Senjary. Just south of Senjary was a series of qalats. Qalats are basically compounds with a number of huts around a field that each family works. There were five or six of these qalats in our area. This was serious indian country. No one had been this far south except the summer before when Navy seals and Afghan commandoes did an air assault and cleared three objectives and RTB (returned to base). Then, in the fall, the 10th Mountain deployed on foot and never even reached Sal Amaka. They got as far as Nashiran and took so many KIA (Killed in Action) and wounded, that they had to leave the area.

This was a Taliban district center with as many as eighty to one hundred twenty enemy fighters. It contained sites for HE (high explosives) and IEDs (improvised explosive devices). Our mission was to air-assault on the southwest side of Sal Amaka and clear it, moving in a northeast direction, allowing Charlie Company to come in from the north. Somehow I knew this was going to be a bad mission. Don't ask me how I knew, I just did. I tidied up my room. I inventoried everything so my Platoon Sergeant would have an easier time getting my things together. I wore my ballistic diaper, to protect my groin area, which usually none of the guys wear. I wore my ear protection and eye protection, the whole nine yards. I was like, "Dude, something bad's gonna happen." I just knew it in my bones.

The night of 24 April, we air assaulted, by Chinook helicopters, to the southwest of Sal Amaka into a poppy field.

We had two platoons. My platoon, 1st platoon, was the assault element and 3rd platoon was the support-by-fire element. We also found out that there were supposed to be TOW missiles set up on a hilltop on the other side of the Arghandab River, but that was cancelled. We believe that the higher-ups weren't cool with the LZ (landing zone). The second thing is that we requested pre-assault fire on our LZs and also on a known HME (homemade explosive) production facility, which also happened to be a foothold on our first objective. Division approved both requests for fire. For whatever reason, Brigade denied them. That was to become quite significant down the road, especially for me.

Anyway, we infiltrated into our positions, both elements, at approximately 0200 hours the morning of 25 April. My element had ANA attached to us and we had 3rd platoon covering us. The plan was to leapfrog from one objective to the next. We would clear it then 3rd platoon would come forward as we cleared the next objective. We were in position to assault by 0330 or 0400 hours.

The other platoon took longer to get into position because they had a canal to negotiate. The initial plan was to begin the assault before first light, but that didn't happen because it took 3rd platoon so long to get into position. Once they reached their position, they found out that they had no clear view to support us. They decided to move closer into a building and along the way they hit a monster IED. The guy who stepped on the pressure plate was an ANA RTO (radio telephone operator). He was immediately vaporized and the 1st Sergeant was also killed, along with a specialist named Neal. Some troops had concussions and the working dog suffered hearing loss. We saw the explosion about two hundred meters away and no one realized the RTO had been killed. It took approximately an hour to assess that the RTO was dead. All they found was his weapon and part of his radio. That delayed us considerably. Finally, 3rd platoon gathered itself and moved into position.

It's now daylight and we begin our assault. First off, we fired a mine-clearing charge. It's a rocket with a one hundred meter tail consisting of C4 explosive that is fired, and when the line is deployed, it is fired, creating a ten by one hundred meter cleared path. We don't walk on any paths, roads, or streets, because of mines. We fired this through a field, then moved forward and blew a hole in the wall of the known HME factory. We found evidence of high explosives, pressure plates, and fuses. The ANA refused to enter the compound; they have become mutinous because of the KIAs and because they had just lost a 1st Sergeant to a suicide bomber on a motorcycle prior to this mission.

Now, at this point, we were right next to the objective. Our eyes overhead hadn't seen anyone on the objective, so we knew this was going to be a gigantic conflict, ambush, house borne IED. Once again, we request fire on the building, and once again we are denied. Inside we find tea that is still warm, signs that the bad guys were eating here, sleeping here, and manufacturing bombs here.

At this point we move forward, blasting our way through everything, throwing line charges in front of us. There's a gate that opens into the main compound and a line of mulberry trees to the right, and past that, a poppy field. To the left are a three-story tower and the bomb-making factory we just left. As we near the gate, I see a set of 7.62x54R bullets nailed into a mulberry tree, usually a clue to the locals that there was a booby trap in that area. To the left, thrown up in the tree branches, was a motorcycle battery charger, a pretty strong indicator that there was an IED there. Also, there was a bag full of ALN (aluminum nitrate) and a big metal dish.

Okay, so we cleared it with the Vallon, (mine detector) and the dog. The ANA commander is flipping out at this point because he's scared. You can see it in his eyes. Mind you, Captain Torhan Aminullh was one of the best officers I ever worked with in any Army. He was solid. He was the ANA commander, the Afghan commander. He's so angry; he's terrified. He's so angry with his guys that he takes a Vallon, a shitty little metal detector and moves on down the road just to show his guys, you know, pussies, and starts walking down the road. So we clear the intersection and I have my guys move forward.

We started to clear the compound and I noticed my radio battery started to die. Oh shit. Mind you, I've been on one hundred patrols in Afghanistan at this point, and on every one of them I had a spare radio battery in my right side pouch. Not this time. So right before my radio died, I tell my company commander, "Sir, we need to drop a bomb on this objective." Once again, Brigade denies it. I'm like, "fuck, somebody's gonna die." I take two steps back toward the compound and BOOM. I get blown up. Right in an area we had just cleared, right where the indicators were.

I found out later that it was a fifty pound jug of homemade explosives with one-and-a-half-inch ball bearings in it. Fortunately, the person who detonated it did not set off the main charge. Only God knows why. I shouldn't be alive right now. I lost my foot and lower right leg. The ball bearings traveled along my arm up to my shoulder. A couple of my guys received concussions.

So, I was lying there; I knew my leg was gone and I could feel darkness. Darkness starts creeping at the edge of your vision, and your vision starts tunneling. I was looking at my leg, and there was arterial blood pouring out of it in a big puddle around me. I was lying there in the street and my first thought was to take my left hand and reach into my pants to make sure my genitals were intact, and they were. So I said, "alright, I wanna live, I wanna live." The fact that I had my manhood gave me the will to live. I put a tourniquet on myself. Then I sat up and I yelled, "Is everybody okay?"

At this point I was not scared; I was angry and pissed. I started laughing and joking with my guys and just basically bullshitting with them. Then our medic (Doc Gardner) rushes up and starts cutting my clothing off. I'm clutching photos of my girlfriend. The medic sticks an IV in my arm and hits it the first time. So I'm laughing because the EOD (explosives ordinance disposal) guy is holding my hand and it's the hand I had just grabbed my balls with. We're all laughing and joking about that and it was good because I didn't want my guys freaking out about what had just happened.

So they get me on a litter and take me over to a poppy field. The medevac lands, they load me on it, and they pump me full of something and I pass out. At some point during the flight I was told I bled out. My heart stopped and they somehow managed to get blood back into me and start my heart. I had some pretty bizarre, vivid hallucinations, either that, or I was headed toward the afterlife. I'm not a particularly religious person. It was a very strange experience. I saw the tunnel, the white light that is so common, and started walking towards it, the whole nine yards. It was weird, but I don't want to get into all my hallucinations and shit. I was told we generated fifteen Purple Hearts on that mission.

I was flown to Khandahar, and then a few days later to Bahgram, where I stayed on an extra day so they could pump blood into me because of the massive loss of blood I experienced. From there I was flown to Landstuhl, Germany for three days, and from there I came home to Walter Reed Hospital. I can tell you that was the worst experience of my life, the flight from Germany to Walter Reed in a C-17. I would happily get blown up again rather than do that flight again. I was up on the 2nd level and for some unknown reason, I could not void my bladder. I tried to piss, but only a little would come out and I was in immense pain. Finally, one of the crew members came by and helped me to the bathroom and held me up so I could urinate while standing, and that was a little bit better. The aircrew tried their best to make me comfortable but it defies description just how painful that flight was.

I will be here at Bethesda, Walter Reed Hospital for six to

nine months. My 1st Sergeant came to visit me here and told me to stay strong. My response was, "1st Sergeant, if I was gonna roll over and die, I would have done it in Afghanistan." From here I would like to go to SFAS (Special Forces Assessment and Selection). That's the track I was on before I got blown up. There's already been one amputee who has been selected for Special Forces. So, that's kind of my plan right now. That said, if I don't get selected for SF, I'll probably leave the Army. My family does not want me to stay in the Army; however, my Dad says he will support me in whatever I choose. My Mom definitely does not want me to stay in; she did not want me to join the Army in the first place. I will keep as many irons in the fire as I can. Only time will tell.

5

I NEVER KNEW SKIN COULD HANG OFF A BODY LIKE THAT

My name is Leon Brimm. I am thirty-six years old at the time of this writing, and I live in Bristol, Tennessee. I was born and raised in the small town of Bristol and will probably stay here the rest of my life. I joined the Army National Guard in 1998 after a struggle with some enlistment problems with the Navy. Seems I had too many speeding tickets. Army slots for the MOS, (military occupational specialty) I wanted were full, so I decided to wait. My neighbor was a recruiter and suggested I join the National Guard. That way I could see how much I liked Army life, but on a part time basis. I agreed and signed up with the Tennessee's 278th Armored Cavalry Regiment as a 19D Cavalry Scout.

Basic training and advanced training were combined for that particular job. This was known as OSUT (one station unit training). In other words it was basic combined with scout school. But to me it was more like sixteen weeks of pure torture. I did my initial training at Fort Knox, Kentucky with D-Troop, 5-15 Cav., 3rd Platoon Panthers. On a side note, if anyone ever tells you they were in the service and they cannot remember exactly what unit they were in during basic, go ahead and walk away because they are not being truthful.

I ended up serving ten years in the National Guard, but two of those years were on active duty during Operation Iraqi Freedom III. That was my first and only deployment overseas. My troop was detached from the main body of the 278th out of Tennessee, and my troop (Troop F 2/278th), was initially placed under the command of 3/8 Cavalry in Baghdad, Iraq under the banner of Taskforce Baghdad. This eventually changed because 3/8 moved back to stateside and was replaced with 4/64 Armor (Tuskers, 3rd Infantry Division), who we continued to serve under until we remobilized back to Kuwait.

On Labor Day, 2005 I was working in conjunction with the US Navy Special Warfare EOD (explosive ordnance disposal). My job as a Cavalry Scout was to dismount when we came upon an IED (Improvised Explosive Device) and pull security as needed for the EOD team to place charges on the IED and remove the threat, usually by exploding it. This day did seem somewhat different, due to the fact that we were just a few weeks from going home and the fact that we were out of our normal AO (area of operation). I think, well, I knew, I had a weird feeling before we even loaded up to roll. As we were approaching the target area, all I remember is the smell of fire and burning rubber. I never heard the explosion and really don't remember much after the fact for what seemed like ten minutes or more. I was knocked unconscious, received burns to my face and my hands, and I apparently inhaled at just the right time for the fire ball to burn my esophagus and lungs. I only found this out after chest x-rays at the hospital because I was having a hard time breathing.

The guys in the vehicle with me were Sergeant Chris Cartwright, Specialist Jamie Smith, Lieutenant L.C. and Abe, our interpreter. Behind us was the Navy EOD team, one medical vehicle, and in the rear was the other security hummer from our unit. Sergeant Cartwright and I were the least wounded. Specialist Smith took extensive shrapnel to the neck and face. Abe basically had all the skin burned off both of his arms. I never knew skin could hang off a body like that. The Lieutenant suffered a concussion and his hands were badly burned.

Once the vehicle stopped rolling, the first to help us out were a couple of medics who were assigned to us by 3rd Infantry Division. I cannot remember their names, and that's sad, but one got me off the ground and away from the burning hummer. I'm not exactly sure what the other medic did, but I do know he was assisting in the welfare of other wounded soldiers. Once the situation was somewhat settled and I came to, I was able to help again. I went back to the truck and helped remove maps, radios, weapons, and sensitive items. Then, I was called by the medics to help stabilize Specialist Smith. They wanted me to hold a pressure dressing on his neck while they attended to Abe and the Lieutenant.

Around the same time, the hummer was still burning and the leftover rounds in the vehicle started to "cook off." And now our hummer was letting loose with 7.62 mm rounds in all directions. Ultimately, we had to take cover, and at the same time figure out what we were going to do. Sergeant Cartwright was asking for a med flight and other options of extraction for

Smith, the Lieutenant, and Abe, but we did not have time to sit in the middle of the city and wait.

One has to imagine, one vehicle destroyed, three seriously wounded men, two slightly wounded, and only one gun truck to protect the rest of us while we stood in the open on a bright sunny day looking at hundreds of Iraqis slowly walking up to the scene. At this point I could not find my M-4, but I had a pistol, so I pulled it out and waited. I guess I was either waiting for a firefight or for an order to leave. About that time, Sergeant Brad Slagle from the rear gun truck handed me my M-4 and then I heard it, just barely, because my ears were still ringing, but a couple of Blackhawks and a small platoon from 3rd ID just a few blocks away, assisted in securing the area.

This made the spectators back off and we decided to just load up the wounded in the med truck, leave the wrecked truck and disperse back to the Green Zone and get our injured guys into the hospital. This plan turned out to be successful and Specialist Smith and the Lieutenant were both stabilized and sent on to Germany, and later, back to the States. Abe, on the other hand, was hospitalized for severe burns to both arms, and I have no idea what ever became of him. I do know that he was very brave, was wounded multiple times before working with us, and really thought America could help spread freedom to Iraq. He was a true patriot of his country.

After all that was taken care of, Sergeant Cartwright and I were placed on ten days of down time. We had to attend a group counseling session with the rest of the guys who were on the mission, minus Smith and the Lieutenant. After ten days of down time, I was reassigned to 2nd platoon where we did checkpoint duty on night shift. Sergeant Cartwright went back to EOD security until the mission ended a couple of weeks later.

I received my Purple Heart in what I would call a semi-private ceremony. Usually, when you get an award, you are called up in front of everyone; but we (Sergeant Cartwright, me, and two guys I did not know) stood in front of Colonel Cordon, the 1st Sergeant, and other officers to receive our Purple Heart awards at FOB (forward operating base) Prosperity in 2005. They asked us all how we felt and I just said, "I'm glad I am alive." That seemed to get some laughs around the room, but I was serious.

Recently, I just finished my Bachelor's degree in Political Science from King College in Bristol, Tennessee. Now I am preparing to go to graduate school at ETSU in Johnson City, Tennessee to study Political Administration. I want to focus on working with nonprofit organizations that are linked with veterans or the VA (veteran's administration) in order to help veterans transition back into normal life after combat, and help them land a decent job or get the benefits they deserve for serving their country. Hopefully, my vision will come to fruition and my service will be a benefit to those who need help. Let's face it; a veteran understands what other veterans are going through better than someone who has never been involved in that type of life-changing event. I am glad that I served my country.

Thanks to the G.I. Bill and some hard work on my end, one of my goals since combat has been reached, but other goals still remain. I would love to see the support our guys and gals get from everyday civilians actually equate into more than a handshake. Veterans are unemployed at a rate higher than any other group looking for work. This is not fair and it is not right. Instead of just a handshake and a beer for my service, or anyone's service for that matter, I would like to see that handshake accompanied by an opportunity from the private sector, especially to our wounded veterans who are even more challenged to find employment. Make no mistake, I appreciate everyone's service; we are the one percent, but wounded veterans could use a little more help from us all.

RIP Stephen Maddies, Baghdad, Iraq 2007.

6

He Looked Like
Darth Vader

My name is Jared Lemon and I am from Anchorage, Alaska. I joined the Army in 2006. I was a Boy Scout and an Eagle Scout. I always wanted to be a soldier, since I was a kid, I guess. I was twenty-five and figured it was now or never, and chicks dig a guy in uniform, right?

I was asked, "why Airborne," and my answer was, "why not." I'm kind of adventurous and like to do crazy things. I originally joined as an 18 X-Ray, a Green Beret Baby. One day I was having car trouble, so I called in and I was told it would be okay. But, two days later I got called into the First Sergeant's office and was told I was being dropped because the numbers were too high; there were too many applicants for Special Forces. To tell you the truth, I'm glad I ended up in the 82nd Airborne Division because it is a very prestigious unit.

I took my basic training, my infantry training, and my jump training all at Fort Benning, Georgia. I have been in the Army just about six years. My first deployment was to Ghazni Province, Afghanistan, RCE (regional command east). We were based near a town called Nawa. I was there approximately five or six months. While I was there I was a Private and was a gunner on a Hummer. I fired different weapons including the Browning M2 .50 caliber, SAW (squad automatic weapon) that fires the 5.56mm round, and the M240 machine gun which fires the 7.62mm NATO round.

My second deployment was to Helmand Province, Afghanistan. I had been promoted along the way and was now a Sergeant. We were there about four to five months. We worked along with ANCOP which means Afghan National Civil Order Police. I was a rifleman; my basic weapon was the M4 carbine which fires the 5.56mm round, and I eventually became a team leader.

After the first few months in Helmand Province, a Striker Brigade, the 117th out of Seattle, Washington, had lost around thirty guys in their first couple of months. So, we were pulled out of Helmand Province and sent to Kandahar Province. We set up OPs (observation post) and there was a curfew in this area, so any of the locals who were out after the curfew were probably bad guys.

One night we were out patrolling, staying off roads because of mines and IEDs. We crossed fields, went over walls, through orchards, walking single file. We got to this one wall, and I was the tenth man in the eleven man formation, with Sergeant Caron in the last position. I was the team leader. This particular wall was about chest high and a foot in thickness. I had my M4 and some of the extra team equipment. I didn't want our machine gunner overloaded. As the team leader, I didn't want anyone carrying more than their fair share.

So, I climbed over the wall then I turned around to grab

the machine gun from the gunner. After he negotiated the wall I handed him back his gun. I then started looking to see where the rest of my guys were, so I looked for their IR (infrared) strobes that we wore on our helmets. I saw the flashes from the IR strobes and headed out towards them and came upon a tree. I wasn't sure which side of the tree my guys went around, so I figured they went to the left of it because it was farther to go to the right. The reason I was concerned about that was because we had been finding trip wires. So I took two steps, and it seemed like a split second when I heard this ping sound, kind of like when someone takes an aluminum bat and hits a metal pole. The next thing I remember was I had no more green vision from my night vision goggles, my hearing was all muffled, debris and dirt were falling all around me. I was looking up at the sky and my brain was not functioning. Then I heard someone moaning and all of a sudden I realized we had been in an explosion.

I started yelling for help and my best friend, Chad Stewart, who was Alpha team leader (I was Bravo team leader) ran all the way back from the front of the formation to assist. My SAW gunner set off the booby trap and was blown in half. I was thrown in the air and got hit with shrapnel. My buddy shone a red light on me and I could see a big gash really high on my right shoulder. My buddy pushed my head away. I really didn't think I was hurt all that bad. They started performing first aid on me. The main thing that popped into my head was, "How are my guys doing?"

I heard my squad leader saying, "He's gone." I didn't know

who at the time. I heard someone on the radio calling for urgent surgical help and that we had a KIA (killed in action). After that I started focusing on not going into shock myself. It's kind of crazy what you remember. They cut away my clothing and removed my helmet, and I remember helping them take off my falcon rig, which is a harness that holds all my ammo, a knife, emergency first aid gear, and other items. Then they got me into a fetal position.

Finally, the Blackhawk helicopter arrived with Air Force para jumpers on board to medevac me out. So the guys got me up and assisted me in walking out to the chopper. My arm felt really heavy and I realized at that point that it was pretty jacked up. My adrenaline was high and I was close to shock, along with losing a lot of blood.

They got me out to the chopper and I remember sitting down on the edge of it, and then they rolled me into a fetal position once again and put a pillow under my head. I recall seeing the crew chief with his helmet on and he looked like Darth Vader. The last thing I remember is Darth Vader stabbing me with a needle and boom; I was out for four days in a drug-induced coma.

They determined later that the booby trap was either a Russian or Chinese made anti-personnel mine along with some improvised explosives made up in a jug filled with ammonium nitrate, fertilizer, and aluminum powder which makes the explosion much bigger.

They flew me to Khandahar first and performed emergency surgery on me, and two days later they transported me to

Bahgram. A few days later I was on a plane to Germany. They had to land in Germany prematurely because the volcano had erupted in Iceland and all flights were grounded. We stayed there for about two weeks before they could fly me out to Walter Reed Bethesda.

The blast produced a high compound fracture on my right arm, my tricep was gone, my bicep was almost all gone, my forearm was shredded, and it looked like someone took a shotgun to my shoulder. I also had a half dollar size chunk of shrapnel in my ass. Because of the way I was thrown into the air, it looked like someone took an industrial sandblaster to the back of my neck. I had shrapnel in my left ear, my left eardrum was blown out, and I had shrapnel in my temple.

Initially they reattached my arm and for about a month and a half they monitored its progress with an ultrasound machine. The blood was going into my arm and down to my hand but it wasn't flowing properly on the return trip and my arm was getting swollen and sore. So they were pumping blood out of my arm and I had numerous transfusions.

After a month and a half, I couldn't move my hand or feel my hand. I was told there are basically three nerves that control your arm and I was missing a thirteen inch segment in one and a fourteen inch segment in another, and they couldn't repair those. They told me that even if they were able to save my arm, it would just hang there and do nothing.

Finally, the doctors told me they felt it would be to my benefit to remove my arm and start the healing process to where I could get a prosthetic. There were a bunch of doctors in my room, some I had never even seen before, but they had something to do with my case. The ones I didn't know cared for me while I was unconscious and they were all nodding their heads in affirmation that I needed to have my arm removed. My whole family was there too. What the heck, they knew more than I did, so I figured there's no reason to draw this out any longer.

The doctors discussed using my forearm bone to replace what I had lost in my shoulder area, but they never did that. They replaced some veins and did skin grafts, but everything they were doing was not working. This went on for about a little over a year.

Last Memorial Day, 2011, I attended Rolling Thunder and there was a bunch of bikers there and I got to talking with another wounded veteran. I told him I had this wound that wouldn't close and he told me about using magnets. He explained to me that because there's iron in your blood, these magnets help circulate your blood, so he gave me a sock with magnets in it to put over my wound and a necklace with magnets to place on my spine. I did what he told me and two weeks later I was healed, I mean completely healed. I was totally amazed that they didn't have that at Walter Reed.

They tried doing what's called an Apligraf, which is synthetic skin made from harvested infant foreskin. They did three of these on me and the first one fell off, and the other two, my body absorbed them. That didn't work. So then they tried some type of honey treatment, bathing it, ultrasound treatment, and silver nitrate applications to clear up any bacteria, but none of it worked. If it weren't for the magnets, well, I just don't know.

Because of the high compound fracture in my arm, my bone was basically just shattered. They said this happens a lot to guys whose systems have been shocked by explosions. So many of the guys coming back from the war who have been blown up are finding out that their body senses that it's time to start growing new bone. It starts growing, but with no rhyme or reason all over the place. There are even bone spurs that stick out from it. The technical term is endochondral ossification.

This started happening to me, and when I went over to wound care, they removed my dressing and said, "Whoa, dude, you got a bone sticking out of your arm."

I said, "What?" So they held up a mirror to show me because it was on the back side of my arm, and there it was, about the size of my pinky nail. It seemed as if I was growing some kind of demon or something. I started having bone grow out in four different places, and calcium is all it is. It has no nerve endings, there's no feeling, and they would just cut the projections off. Then they just had to wait until the bone stopped growing. Some of the guys had to have radiation therapy to stop their bones from growing. Mine stopped on its own. Then they did MRIs on my shoulder and fed images into a computer and came up with a life size resin model of what the bone looked like. It really didn't look like a regular bone; it was more alien looking.

Finally, I was fitted for my prosthesis. The whole process took over two years and at times it was very depressing. It was tough for me to see other soldiers who had worse injuries than me; they were leaving after four or five months and I was still here. Yeah, that got me depressed. I went through anything and everything, but on the positive side, I can say that I never got an infection.

I was presented my Purple Heart by the Commanding General of the 82nd Airborne Division at that time, General James Huggins.

Before entering the Army I was a bench jeweler with four years of professional experience. I started learning about the jewelry trade my senior year in high school. My goal is to eventually open up my own jewelry store back home in Alaska.

Author's Note: I was at Walter Reed National Military Medical Center in Bethesda interviewing Joe Yantz for this book in a conference room on the third floor. As we finished and went out the door, I saw Jared Lemon coming towards us on a Segway wearing a helmet. He stopped and reached into a bag at his feet and pulled out a hand, a hand that looked very realistic. Jared held it out and proclaimed, "This is my new hand."

Joe Yantz grabbed it in a handshake and said, "Glad to meet you."

We all laughed. He told us the hair on the topside was his own and showed us a bare spot on his arm where they shaved it off. I couldn't believe how real it looked.

"So, I take it you've been fitted for a prosthetic?" I asked.

Beaming from ear to ear, Jared stated, "Yes, finally."

7

I Went to War and Garrison Broke Out

My name is Joe Yantz and I'm originally from Sedalia, Missouri. I joined the Army June 7th of 2007. My dad wanted me to join the Navy; his way of thinking was why walk when you can ride. They take care of you and you're involved in less dangerous activities. I always wanted to be a pilot because I used to watch the show, JAG years ago and thought it would be neat to fly. However, I couldn't get into a pilot program because my eyes are too bad.

My next choice was to become a Navy Seal. That didn't pan out because I'm color blind. I figured then that the Navy wasn't meant to be. So, my friend and I decided we would join the Army. It was off to Ft. Benning on June 20th for basic, AIT, and Jump School.

My first and only deployment was in September 2009 to Kandahar Province, Afghanistan. I was a Specialist with Headquarters Co. as a mortar man. The day I was wounded started out as a transportation assignment, which began around 7:00 a.m. We were transporting personnel from COP (company operations post) Terra Nova, up to COP Nolan. You could see one from the other but we had to take the long way around. We had a combination of personnel and supplies. We had troops in contact with the enemy not too far away to the east.

When we arrived at COP Nolan, they were looking for two mortar guys to go out with them because their mortar men were run pretty ragged. So I said, "Okay, I'll go along." My AG (assistant gunner) was carrying the mortar tube. I was carrying a rucksack full of water which was an essential item out there. We also had Air Force EOD (explosives ordnance disposal) with us that we brought from COP Terra Nova. As we started down the path we could hear lots of gunfire coming from the east where our guys were in contact. We were headed in that direction and later on we'd receive pot shots, but no enemy to be seen. We never saw any enemy troops that we could actively engage.

Up until that point it was just roadside bombs going off or the occasional sniper shooting at us and then disappearing, but now we were going to be pretty much face to face with our enemy. It was, to say the least, exciting. As we got closer, we saw the Kiowas flying around making gun runs. We found out that our guys had taken some casualties. A buddy of mine, Justin Loveless, was shot in the face.

We were about ten to fifteen minutes out from COP Nolan and had to negotiate a wall ahead of us. We were walking single file and I was third man in line. The first guy, Hockland, went over the wall, then Brenner, and as I went to go over the wall I stepped over with my right leg and that's when everything went black and I had this floating sensation. I actually thought shit, someone had set something off. I thought it was either the guy ahead of me or the guy behind me.

I had stepped on a pressure plate wired to a Chinese made 105 rocket imbedded into the wall. At least that's what I was told later on. My buddy, Hockland, who was EMT qualified, was the first to reach me. He applied my tourniquet and basically saved my life. The guy ahead of me, Brenner, had his ass burned and suffered TBI (traumatic brain injury). Because of the wall, the guys behind me were not in too bad a shape. The wall directed most of the blast at me and the two guys ahead of me.

The medevac then arrived. It was a Blackhawk with Air Force PJs (parajumpers) on board. They couldn't land because we were in a pomegranate grove so they lowered a medical bag down, then left to recover Loveless who was lying injured in a field where they could land. At that time the second bird came on station and lowered a rescue stretcher that I was placed in and hoisted out.

They flew me out to Kandahar airfield and then to Bahgram airfield. From there they flew me to Landstuhl, Germany where I stayed for three days fighting off an infection. Then I was transported back here to Walter Reed Hospital, and then made the move to Bethesda, which Walter Reed is now a part of. I have been at Bethesda for about two years now. The explosion took my right leg above the knee. I sustained additional wounds to my neck, my face and both hands, and I've had surgery to repair damage to my eardrum.

I woke up initially with my Purple Heart pinned on me but my Battalion Commander and Battalion Sergeant Major came to visit us all and they presented me with one.

My original goal was to stay in the Army and go gold and become an officer. Since my incident, however, my life has changed drastically. I've had the opportunity meet some great people and partake in some amazing experiences. I've met celebrities like Michael Jordan, Michelle Obama, and George W. Bush. I've gone to the U.S. Open, the Inaugural Ball, taken up hunting, and even returned to Afghanistan.

But most importantly are the relationships that I've made, from the girl of my dreams, to reconnecting with members of my family, to the people who have helped me get back out into the world and shown me so much kindness and support (thanks Joe). All this helped in my attempt to stay in the Army; but when I decided that was not the path for me, it helped me to transition into the civilian world. I have since followed that dream girl to Georgia and will be attending college in the fall. I am extremely positive about my future and could never have done it without all the support I have received.

My afterthought about the war is simply that I wish they would let us do our jobs. The infantryman is really good at what he does; just let him do his job and you will like the results. We offer a lifetime warranty. You've heard the term, "I went to war and garrison broke out." Sadly, that's the truth.

8

HEY DOC, I THINK I
NEED A BAND-AID

Hi. My name is Tim Senkowski and I am originally from San Diego, California. My family then moved to Indiana. I joined the Army in 2007 and after completing my basic and infantry training at Fort Benning, Georgia. I was stationed at Fort Drum, New York with the 10th Mountain Division. I joined the army in order to provide better medical assistance and finances for my family. My son is autistic and my wife has rheumatoid arthritis.

I have been in the military for five years and this was my first deployment. I deployed to RC South in Afghanistan, near Kandahar airfield, on 1 April, 2011. We were about an hour north in the Lam District.

On the morning of October 13, 2011 two foot patrols headed out from our base because an IED had gone off the day before, so they were going out there to make sure the insurgents were not planting any more explosives in that area. We rolled out in vehicles behind them carrying supplies, such as building supplies, sandbags, generators, and hescos (wire mesh container filled with dirt and sand, used as barriers). We were carrying different size hescos, 2 ft. by 2 ft. by 2ft., and also 4 ft., 8 ft., and

16 ft. We had supplies for the ANP (Afghan National Police) for their checkpoints. The vehicle behind ours was carrying more personnel and the vehicle in front of ours was transporting a bobcat to help with construction. The vehicle in front of that one was hauling more personnel, mostly ANA and ANP.

Basically, it was a thirty minute walk to our destination. We were originally going to construct a checkpoint right on the road, but then we saw a better position overlooking the entire valley. So the Platoon Sergeant and other high ranking officers decided to reposition the hescos to the top of the hill. They wanted to make sure the position was safe, so a mine detector was sent in to clear the area. Just to be certain that it was okay, they sent in a second mine detector to sweep the area. Then, they sent up a mine detecting dog to clear the area one more time. No one had been in that area before so they were being extra cautious.

The bobcat was sent up to start clearing the position and leveling the ground so we could start building. I went up with my truck and parked it just right so that we could unload the hescos at waist height. I started bringing down the smaller hescos so we could build a perimeter just high enough for the defenders to kneel down and get into a good firing position. We laid all the hescos down and then broke for lunch which took about a good half hour to an hour.

All the guys were relaxing while some others pulled security, then they rotated so everyone had a chance to rest up. When we went back to work, I jumped back into moving hescos with some of the other guys. I was holding one end of the larger hesco and another guy was holding the other end sixteen feet away, and a friend of mine was about four feet on the side of it, steadying it so the bobcat could fill it with dirt.

All of a sudden it felt as if I had fallen asleep. As I came to, it seemed as if the whole Afghanistan experience was all a dream. As my eyes adjusted and I looked around, all I could see was dirt and blood. I couldn't see anything else because I was inside a crater. The explosion blew me straight up and dropped me back inside the crater.

I noticed my right hand was all bloody, and my left hand was behind me, so I started to wiggle my fingers to make sure that I was still alive and not dreaming. I tried to move my left arm but it wouldn't budge. Finally, I was able to swing it around and noticed I could do more with my left arm than my right. That kind of calmed me down, and then I decided to see if I could stand up. There was no way I was going to stand up; I couldn't even gather the energy to budge an inch.

Next, I heard my buddy Dustin who was standing atop the crater and I heard him say, "Oh my God, they got Ski." I could see he was turning pale and put his hands up to his face and start to cry.

So, I yelled out, "Hey Doc, I think I need a Band-Aid."

So Dustin was crying and giggling at the same time he started to put a tourniquet on my right stump. He finished and then put another tourniquet on my left stump. Then he reached into my jacket and pulled out my tourniquets to use on my arms. He gets all four tourniquets on and I hear my other buddy Austin say, "Doc, I need you to come over here and look at one of my guys." So I told Doc to go, that I would be okay because by that time, some of the other guys had come over and they had been through the first responder course, so I felt comfortable with them there. One of them was another buddy named Gunnserhausen.

Doc left to go check on Sancho, which seemed like twenty minutes, and came back. Actually, it was only five minutes. No one would say what happened to Sancho. He was the guy standing four feet away from me and I found out later, unfortunately, he died. The blast threw him over three hundred meters away.

By this time the adrenaline in my body was starting to subside. I was starting to feel the pain, everywhere, and my head was just throbbing. I was doing all I could so as not to scream because all the guys were there and I was trying to remain calm. I was thinking, I'm not gonna let go, I'm not gonna let go. Keep fighting. Because I knew if I let go and lost it, it was only going to crush my guys more.

They got me down the hill and Dustin started to treat my other wounds. The whole left side of my body was a mess. There were wounds Doc couldn't get tourniquets on. My entire left ass cheek was gone. Dustin took off his top and started jamming it into the existing wounds. I had a button embedded in my face. I lost over half the blood in my body. Because I had lost so much blood, my veins were collapsed and so they had to go straight into my sternum to give me blood. There is no doubt that I owe my life to Doc.

They got this narrow ass stretcher for me, not a back board.

We had wider stretchers with us, so I don't know why the hell they brought that back because I'm a big guy. They loaded me onto it and pieces of my right leg dangled over the end, and there was no flesh on my left kneecap. Each time they carried me and then stopped to rest, they were setting the stretcher down on my dangling leg and I still had nerve endings. I was in excruciating pain each time they did this. I told them they had to do something, so they got the leg up on the stretcher and I heard, "Dude, I'm sorry." Then Doc gave me a lollipop. Oh man, I loved those lollipops. They had morphine in them. They were the coolest lollipops, and they just took all the pain away.

Once they called the medevac, it took about an hour for it to get there from Kandahar. They took me right into surgery and I remained at Kandahar for three or four days. They did one operation on what remained of my right leg; my left leg was gone above the knee. The bomb had thrown a lot of debris into my body, so they had to keep cleaning all the junk out of me to keep infection from setting in.

I had seven surgeries before I left Kandahar. My buddy Dustin never left my side. The one and only time he did leave was to identify the body of Sancho. The doctors wanted to amputate my right arm because they said they had never seen an arm injury as bad as mine. My scar goes all the way around my arm where they took out six to eight inches of nerves. My medial nerve is severely damaged; my radial nerve is moderately damaged. I had so many surgeries, I lost count.

I was then flown to Landstuhl, Germany for another surgery on my right leg, and from there I was sent to Bethesda

Walter Reed Hospital where another three surgeries resulted in the loss of my right leg above the knee. I do not remember receiving my first Purple Heart. I was told a Special Forces Colonel pinned it on me. The Purple Heart I received here was given to me by Major General James Huggins.

When I leave here to go home I have land that I will divide. I will use three acres to build a house for my wife and me, along with our two children. Another three acres I will give to my Mother and her husband to build their house. That way they can help us with our needs.

I love the fact that I did what I did in the Army, and if I could, I would stay in. I did not want to come back stateside when I did. I would gladly have pulled guard duty there if they could have put me in a chair with a machine gun. This is a war on terrorism and it needs to be addressed. What I was doing is one way to address this issue; but, there are many other ways. There are always going to be casualties in war, but the best thing people can do is to support the men and women who go forth and carry the fight to the enemy so that the war doesn't come here.

9

Unless the Kid Has Cable TV, I Don't Think It's a Real Grave

My name is Alex Jauregui and I am from a small town named Williams in California. I joined the Army on July 28, 2003. I enlisted because I had enough of school work and basically had nothing better to do. I remember having this one high school teacher who had some military experience and he told me a lot about the military. He said that he thought I'd be good material for the service. I volunteered for airborne because the extra money was good.

My basic training was at Fort Knox, Kentucky because I originally joined to be a mechanic. I was posted to Aberdeen, Maryland where I was an all wheel mechanic. I worked on all types of military vehicles. Because I was airborne qualified, I was sent to Ft. Bragg, North Carolina and assigned to XVIII Airborne Corps. In 2008, I re-classed to infantry and went to Fort Benning, Georgia for basic once more and infantry training. I had completed airborne school right after Fort Knox, so it was back to Fort Bragg, North Carolina, home of the 82nd Airborne Division. I was assigned as an infantryman with Bravo Company, 2/508, with 4th Brigade.

My first deployment was to Baghdad, Iraq with XVIII

Airborne Corps. That was a twelve-month deployment. My second deployment was also to Iraq with XVIII Airborne Corps at Al Taqaddum which is near Fallujah, and that was a fifteen-month stay. My third deployment was to the Arghandab River Valley in Afghanistan, near Kandahar, with 2/508th. That tour lasted another twelve months.

My last deployment was also with 2/508th near the Zhari District. I was there around two months when we were sent out on patrol this particular day. The squad that went out was Sergeant Hammer's squad which was our 2nd squad from Bravo Company, 1st Platoon, of the 508th Parachute Infantry Regiment.

So, Sergeant Hammer took his squad out to a village named Jannon to speak with the village elder about a cache that was found two days before, outside of the mosque, which included mines, a rocket, and explosives. They kept claiming there were no Taliban around but yet we kept finding signs that there were. There was also an IED found a few days prior to this, plus, there was quite a bit of gunfire in this area.

On their way to the village, they found an IED near one of our strong points, basically a checkpoint. I had a five-man team that was approximately 400 to 500 meters away from the discovered IED. Our FSC (forward support company) brought out some EOD guys and we linked up with Sergeant Hammer and Platoon Sergeant Musil, and I asked where they needed me and my team. They told me to cover down the west side, so I set my guys up on that side of the perimeter. Then Sergeant Hammer was able to collapse his squad so we could cover a smaller area. We got all set up and watched as EOD did their thing, exploding the IED.

I remembered Sergeant Musil telling me about a lone grave where they had found the initial cache of explosives. When a local national was questioned about it, he replied that it was some infant's grave. We all thought it was weird but no one really gave it a second thought. Then I asked Sergeant Musil if the grave was facing north to south or east to west. He said he really hadn't taken notice and asked why. I said that traditionally Afghanis bury their dead north to south with the head to the north.

I remembered that discussion so I went looking for that grave. I noticed that the grave was facing east to west, and after moving a few rocks, I exposed some wires. I had discovered a second IED. I took some pictures of it and radioed the information back to command. My exact words were, "Unless the kid has cable TV, I don't think it's a real grave."

EOD had Sergeant Musil set up a safe zone around the IED so they could get started doing their thing and eventually blowing it. Sergeant Musil told me he wanted to see the IED so I pointed him in the direction from where I came and he set off, with me getting ready to follow a few paces behind, always walking in single file because of the constant danger of other mines and booby traps.

I remember, it was only my second step and the next thing I knew my ears were ringing and I said, "Fuck my life." Sergeant Hammer was the first one to get to me and I could see him, but my vision was blurred so I knew that my eyesight wasn't gone. I kept trying to sit up to assess my injuries but Sergeant Hammer kept holding me down.

So, I asked Sergeant Hammer how I was and he said, "You're going to be okay." Then I asked again how I was, and Sergeant Hammer replied, "You're going to be okay, buddy."

I started getting frustrated and said, "Yo, how fuckin' bad is it? Ya know, I would tell you. Is it one leg or both legs?"

Sergeant Hammer said, "Both legs."

I just sort of laid back and they started working on me and I could hear Sergeant Hammer giving instructions to the PFC Miles as to where and how to apply the tourniquets and stuff. I could hear Sergeant Musil calling for a medevac. At that point I was pretty much calm, but then as time passed the pain started and I was screaming for morphine. They gave me morphine and after that kicked in I started saying to Sergeant Hammer, "Why'd I have to walk over there? Why? I was already in the safe zone."

The next thing I knew they were putting me on the bird and I remember PFC Miles boarded the chopper with me. I was starting to lose consciousness. But, as I looked down I saw the sole of my boot pointing towards me so I pretty much knew that leg was done for. As it turned out, the other day I met the guys who medevacked me out, and they said a couple of SF (special forces) guys were in the area that day and they helped load me on the chopper and then went back and got my foot and threw it on the stretcher with me. So, I thought it was attached, but they told me later that it wasn't.

While I was being transported, PFC Miles tried to keep

me conscious by talking to me. But finally, there comes a time when you can no longer talk, so they tell you to blink if you understand. Then I couldn't do that, so they told me to squeeze their finger and I did that, but then I couldn't even do that anymore. Miles would say, "Jauregui, can you hear me? Squeeze my finger." I could hear him but I just couldn't respond to him any longer. At one point I was able to reach out and grab the SF guy's leg and told him I needed morphine. I remember hearing one of the SF guys yelling that we were two minutes out and that's probably what saved me. From the time the chopper was called until the time I was in the Kandahar hospital, it took approximately 20 minutes.

The incident happened around 1400 hours on Easter Sunday, 2011. I was treated there and hours later I was flown to Bahgram where I spent the next day and from there I was transported to Landstuhl, Germany, where I spent five days. I was then flown to Bethesda Walter Reed Hospital.

I was told later on that they thought the bomb was a twenty pound IED. I do know that there was a pressure plate wired to a jug of HME (homemade explosives) consisting of ammonium nitrate, aluminum powder, and fertilizer.

I lost my left leg just below the knee which is an ideal amputation if you have to have one. My right leg has a disarticulation, which is through the knee, meaning I still have my kneecap. That has its advantages and disadvantages. The advantage is that I still have my kneecap, which is good for weight bearing. There was no amputation into my femur, and my femur is already used to bearing that weight. The disadvantage is that my right knee is lower than my left knee, so I have this hip bobbing thing going on. So, I have to learn how to walk to reduce the hip bobbing problem.

I had my third and fourth digits on my right hand amputated at the first joint. I had injuries to both my eyes in that there was a little shrapnel in them, but it wasn't too serious. At first they had to give me steroid drops in my left eye for about a month. My right eardrum is completely blown out and my left eardrum has some extensive damage. A lot of times when there is damage to the ears, they tend to heal themselves; but in my case surgery will be required and that is going to happen in the very near future. I have shrapnel and burn scars on my right arm and I have a wound that goes from my right knee up to my waist which was basically just a hole.

I was sort of upset because it was approximately a month before anyone from the 82nd came to see me. Finally, I was told that Major General Huggins had stopped by and presented me with my Purple Heart. I must have been out of it because I didn't recall seeing him, but that really made my day hearing that.

I'll spend about eighteen months here doing rehab and then I'm not sure where I'll go from here or what I will do. I love the Army and our organization. I have an outstanding platoon sergeant and really good squad leaders, and I was very fortunate in that respect. But, I don't see me staying in my present unit. I may be able to change my MOS. I have a few options, the main one is going back to school, me and my wife, and perhaps working in my brother's factory. As a last resort, someone suggested that I could always be a mechanic.

10

MAY, INJURED IN MAY

Hello, my name is May Agurto and I am from the Bronx, New York. I joined the Army in January 2008. I joined the military basically to just get away from everything in the Bronx. I desperately needed a change.

I went to Fort Leonard Wood for my basic training and then trained with the Seabees to get my 12 Whiskey (masonry and carpentry) MOS. After completing my training, I went back to New York as a member of the 668th Engineer Company.

I deployed to Afghanistan in the Kandahar Province area in December of 2011. Our main mission was to pave the roads because when it rained it made the roads extremely muddy and difficult for the troops to maneuver on. We would put up about three or four inches of dirt and then cover that with crushed rock. On May 1, 2012 we were told that the area we were working in was a hot spot, so all the small machinery and equipment was removed from the flatbeds.

We had two dump trucks and I was in one of them with my driver, Foraker. We made a few trips back and forth with dirt until my platoon sergeant told us to stop because the cable from the winch, on the front of the truck, had come loose and tangled around the tire. They had a tough time unraveling the cable but finally they had it loose and were about to connect it to the vehicle in front of ours so we could roll it back onto the winch. That's when the Taliban fired an RPG(rocket-propelled grenade) and hit our truck. The rocket came through my door on the passenger side and went into the dash board.

I wasn't exactly sure what had just happened, so I looked out the window and saw my platoon sergeant crouched behind some rocks, and then I looked back at Foraker and he was bleeding and sort of spaced out. Then I started to feel the pain and they got me out of the truck and I was kind of flapping my arms because I was so excited. They told me to calm down and I did, but I didn't want to look down at my legs. I was afraid to. The pain was intense.

I was medevacked out to Kandahar, then to Bahgram, and from there to Landstuhl, Germany. I arrived in Bethesda around the 7th of May.

I had severe damage to my left leg and damage to my right leg and my left hand. I had burns on my right hand. The doctors had to remove some large pieces of shrapnel from my left leg and sew it up. Then they discovered I had DVT (deep venous thrombosis) in my left leg. That's a blood clot that forms in the vein. They put me on some medication for it and are hoping blood thinners will dissolve the clot. If not, they will put a type of filter in the vein above the clot so the clot won't be able to move. I also have blurred vision and a blind spot in my right eye. I have nerve damage in the left ear and a ruptured eardrum in my right ear. The doctors plan on cutting around the back of my ear and flapping it over to make the repair, and then they'll sew it back on. I also have some TBI (traumatic brain injury).

I plan on returning to my unit in New York. I have already re-enlisted and would very much like to make a career out of the Army. The next step for me is to apply for drill sergeant school. If that doesn't pan out then I will probably go into teaching. I would have to go to school first and then I would like to teach art and sign language.

I'm glad I did what I did and served my country. I got to build guard towers, latrines, and a house. We built offices and put in the shelving, entertainment centers, showers and all that stuff. You name it; we built it to make the troops' lives more comfortable. If we had enough wood, we'd build something. I was a squad leader, a specialist, in charge of four men. Sometimes other units would get skeptical of me, being a woman, but then they wound up always wanting us because we get the job done.

11

Oh No, Not Again

My name is Dave Smith and I am from Rocky Mount, West Virginia. I joined the Army on 20 June, 1990. I joined the Army because as a young boy I just knew I wanted to be a part of the military. I took my basic training at Fort Jackson, South Carolina, and my advanced training at Fort Gordon, Georgia. I went to airborne school in December of 1990 at Fort Benning, Georgia. An hour before we graduated jump school, they called a formation and called out fifty names and told us to remain. The rest of the graduating class was told they could go on leave.

We were taken into a classroom and told we would be receiving all our gear and be reporting to our units in Saudi Arabia. They were gearing up for the Gulf War. When I arrived in the desert, I reported to my unit, which was the 82nd Airborne Division, Signal Battalion, on 15 January, 1991, the day the air war kicked off. I was attached to 82nd aviation.

My time there was quite uneventful because, as we know, the Iraqis didn't take to the bombing very well and they were surrendering in droves. Most of my time there was spent doing my commo (Communications) job. I was there approximately five months as a private. I returned to Fort Bragg and spent around nine years there with the 82nd signal battalion. My main job while I was there was to jump radios with and for the infantry brigades, mostly with the 505th and I enjoyed that assignment.

During that time, I had a few reenlistments and attempted to get assigned to a long range surveillance detachment. That didn't pan out. I tried reenlisting to get assigned to one of the infantry units in the 82nd by changing my MOS, or to get assigned somewhere else. None of that worked for me, so in February 1999, I ETSd (expiration term of service) out of the Army. I left the military as an E-5 Sergeant.

I bounced around at a few jobs for around six months and at that time Kosovo, Bosnia, and Serbia were big in the news. I had a few friends still in the military who were involved in those areas, so I talked it over with my wife, we had a young daughter at the time, and I decided to go back into the Army.

I knew I didn't want to return to Fort Bragg because I needed something different, so the recruiter made it possible to be assigned to Germany. While I was there I met a friend from Bragg who was with the 10th Special Forces in Stuttgart. He spoke to me about the possibility of me coming into his unit because it was one of only two jump units in Germany. I agreed and he went and spoke to one of the company sergeant majors in Charlie Company, 10th Group.

I had to send him a resume describing all of my prior military experience. My application was accepted and I reported to Charlie Company, 1st Battalion, 10th Special Forces Group.

Once I got there I realized there was life in other places in the Army. The 82nd was a great place to grow up and I don't regret one minute of the time I spent there. When I was in the 82nd, I believed there was the 82nd Airborne Division and then, everybody else. When I got to the 10th, I saw that there were other units doing great things.

I was attached to the B Team in Charlie Company as a commo guy, and I met some terrific NCOs and officers there. These guys were top shelf, and seeing what they do, I thought, who wouldn't want to do this? I mean, they blow in doors, do entries, shoot stuff up, and, the one thing that motivated me was that training took a back seat to nothing. Training was the end all, be all. Anything that had anything to do with something other than training for combat, it got taken care of later, by some other guys. Being on the B Team, I was one of those other guys, but I understood that. I knew my role on the team and our NCO instilled in us that the Team comes first and we needed to support them in our role.

So, it was around August of 1999 and we went out to several locations throughout Europe for training. On 11 September, 2001 we were actually on a training mission in Romania and it was very surreal to have something of that proportion happen and be part of a unit like the 10th Special Forces. At the time we thought it was part a training exercise, until they brought out a TV and we saw the second tower fall. I had a lump in my throat and knew, at that moment, that everything had changed. I had already been training up to go to selection at that time, and 9/11 made my mind up for me and my buddy whom I spoke of earlier.

In November I left for SFAS (Special Forces assessment selection) at Ft. Bragg where you are pushed to the limit for three weeks. At the end of those three weeks, selections are made. We had 270 soldiers who started the selection course and out of that 150 finished. Out of the 150 who finished, about 120 were finally selected. By being selected, that meant I was accepted for Special Forces training.

I then returned to Germany. Shortly thereafter orders were cut for me to return to Ft. Bragg at the John F. Kennedy Special Warfare School. I started the Special Forces qualification course in April, 2002 and finished in September 2003. Much of the training takes place at Camp McCall, near Ft. Bragg. My specialty training took place at Ft. Bragg and that was communications, as well as language school, which in my case was French. I completed my training, which was about a year and a half, and in October, 2003 I was assigned to 1st Battalion, 3rd Special Forces Group at Ft. Bragg.

I got to my team and found out that they had just returned from their first OEF (operation enduring freedom) deployment in Afghanistan. We are now preparing for what will be my first rotation in January 2004. We're doing all kinds of training, and I'm learning what my real job is, not just what they teach you in the qualification course.

So I'm now on my first deployment to Afghanistan, and back then the insurgency wasn't like now, it wasn't fully matured yet. They were still reeling from the ass kicking they had taken during the initial invasion.

I was involved in five trips to Afghanistan. On my third rotation, our team had just completed a large scale offensive operation with the Canadians of the NATO forces. We were basically sent out to occupy a piece of real estate called Panjawai in the Kandahar Province, in southern Afghanistan. This was a significant area strategically, in that we were the first ever NATO led operation in Afghanistan. This was in August or September of 2006. The result of our being there was the curtailing of a large scale attack by the Taliban on the city of Kandahar.

The number of Taliban in the area was greatly exaggerated and we ended up killing around 500 to 600 enemy fighters. After that, we began rotations between our team and another team. Our objective was to increase the overall space and increase Afghan government influence. On 6 November, 2006 we had just finished one of our two week stints, getting ready to switch out with our other team.

I was now the intelligence sergeant, having moved over from commo, and I knew and briefed the team that what the Taliban were going to do was to attempt to seal us into our compound on this hilltop called Spear 1 GAR, gar meaning mountain in Afghan, which sits among densely populated villages. The enemy was going to attempt to keep us isolated, from getting support, and from expanding our influence. Prior to the big offensive earlier, we sat for three days and watched, literally, thousands of civilians leave the area because they knew a fight was coming. So, by November of that year, the entire area was devoid of inhabitants. There were no families. It gives you a kind of eerie feeling as you're walking through those villages and they're absolutely empty of people. We knew that the only people still there were fighters.

We had just finished doing a hand over to our other team, giving them a briefing as to what we had accomplished and what the situation was at that time, and showing them some infrastructure we had built on the hillside. When we finished, my team got into the vehicles to leave. I was in the number two vehicle in a four-vehicle convoy. I was the driver of our vehicle, and I had a team member in the passenger seat and another team member in the top turret. We were driving GMBs (ground mobility vehicles) basically the original Humvees, without all the up armor. They are a Special Forces version with a beefed up suspension, more powerful turbo engine, and a much better transmission. The only armor on them is in the seats and the doors. We would take Kevlar blankets and put them on the floors, to provide a bit more protection.

We took off, it was dark, around four o'clock in the morning. The area to our south, between where the ANA (afghan national army) and the Canadian forces were located had experienced around thirty IED attacks in the last month. There was a route to the north that we found out about that hadn't been used much. We did a good deal of dismounted patrols in that area to make sure it was safe because we knew we'd be using it in a few days.

We got about two clicks away from Spear 1 Gar, and we were going around a turn with a four foot wall on the passenger side and a twelve foot wall on the driver's side, with room enough for just one Humvee. I remember this big bright light, and I knew immediately we had hit an IED. To this day, and everything else I had been through, it was the most violent episode I had ever experienced. After years of training, breeching doors, concussion grenades, firing rounds, and anything else I can think of, this was THE single most violent thing I can remember. We learned later on that a pressure plate set the IED (an anti-tank mine) off, and it detonated under the right passenger side tire. It left a crater in the ground about four to five feet deep by about three feet wide.

My initial feeling was that I had been blown back over the seat, because when I came to, I noticed the seat was over my legs. However, the blast pushed me entirely out of the vehicle about twenty feet. My legs were lying across the sight for the Mark 47, which is a mounted grenade launcher and machine gun combination that was on the turret.

Prior to leaving in the convoy, I was having a debate with myself about my driver door. In our community we have a rule that says, "Shooter's choice," which means you may improvise. Some of our guys preferred to have their doors latched in the open position for better range of motion and fire. My door had a malfunction in that, if I closed it, the latch stuck and I would have a hard time opening it. I needed someone else to open the door from the outside. My role, as a driver, is to drive and concentrate on the road. I decided to close my door, but not latch it. I think that decision probably saved me from more severe injuries. Because my door was only partially latched, it allowed me to be thrown out of the vehicle, whereas if the door remained latched completely, I would have been injured more.

We were driving with NODs (night observation devices), and that is why I remembered seeing such a bright flash.

When I initially came too, I went into auto pilot and I remember that there was dead silence, not a sound could be heard. Then my thought was that the enemy was about to open up with the ambush. The vehicle, which weighed about 10,000 lbs, was picked up by the explosion, turned ninety degrees, and it sat right on that four foot wall. My buddy in the passenger seat was still in the Humvee with the vehicle basically wrapped around him. My gunner, in the turret, was blown out of the vehicle, back onto the road.

Initially, the team had trouble finding me; they didn't know where I was. I was lying in this field, thinking an attack was forthcoming, flat against the ground and reaching for my M4 rifle, and I realized that it's in the vehicle. So I pull out my pistol from my leg holster and I waited to see muzzle flashes from the tree line. I finally realized there was no ambush coming.

Then I heard my other team members yelling and I thought that I must be missing something after that huge explosion. I start reaching down my legs, checking my arms, and all I could see was some blood on my left hand. My nose was bleeding and my chest hurt from the over pressure from the IED. My knees and ankles were pretty banged up. I crawled up to the Humvee, and from the windshield forward, there was nothing. I could see inside and it was just a black mess of twisted metal around the guy in the passenger seat.

We called for medevac from Kandahar and after they were able to extricate my buddy from the vehicle, they loaded him into one of the Blackhawks. But I found out later that he was already dead. My other team member and I went out on a second Blackhawk. When we got to Kandahar, our Colonel and Sergeant Major were there waiting and helped get us into the hospital for treatment.

I had severe damage to my ankles, a cracked sternum, a broken nose, tore my PCL on my right knee, and some tissue damage to my left knee as well. They treated me there at Kandahar and, ultimately, I stayed in country and returned to my firebase near Kandahar City, which was Firebase Maholic, named after MSG Tom Maholic, who was killed in the same area where we hit the IED. His death was one of the reasons we did that initial big offensive where 500-600 enemy fighters were killed.

My gunner and I decided our injuries didn't warrant us leaving the country, so we went back to our team. It took about a month until I recovered from my injuries. My biggest problem was walking because of the injuries to my ankles. My gunner recovered a bit sooner than I.

The beginning of January, 2007 I went on my first patrol since my injuries. I needed to do that; I needed to get back on that horse. Otherwise, I'd be completely useless as an SF guy. That first patrol, I saw IEDs everywhere, but that was good for me. My team leader Rusty, and Colonel Bolduc, were both good at pushing me, but not pushing too hard. They knew I needed this. After a few patrols, I started getting my confidence back.

I came back to the states in March of 2007 to Ft. Bragg and went through Womack Army Hospital where they checked me out. Basically, there was nothing they could do for the torn PCL. The right knee healed awkwardly. They ended up cutting the Achilles on my left foot and extending that. They put some screws in the top of my left foot, and also in my heel, because it had shifted about a quarter of an inch. That's about it other than I did experience some TBI. I received a Purple Heart which was awarded to me by my SF team. That was my third Afghanistan deployment.

My fourth trip to Afghanistan was several years later in June of 2010. I'm now a platoon sergeant. We were headed to Helmund Province in the Sangin District. We knew from other SF teams there that this was a bad place; there was no white space (an area free of insurgents) whatsoever. They were getting direct and indirect fire right onto the firebase, and suicide bombers hitting the gate. The only people there were the SF team, four civilians, six ANA soldiers, and a company of United Arab Emirate assault commandos.

This was Firebase Robinson, and from what we saw, it needed quite a bit of improvements. First off, the water was undrinkable and unusable for bathing because there were feces and e-coli in it. There was very little perimeter security up. There were gaps one hundred yards long in places. The base was about four miles around. It was a rather large area to control for the amount of personnel we had.

Because we were in Helmund Province, we fell under southeast command which was the Marines. The Marines and the Brits shared this area. We had a bit of a problem getting support from the Marines, but we worked it out. We had a plan, a good plan to implement afghan government action; however, the insurgent problem there was the worst I had ever seen. There was no security there for the people, so they had no choice but to support the insurgency.

We had been at the firebase about one month. On the eastern side of it there is just open desert. On the western side of the firebase is part of the Helmund River, where it is lush and green and thick, which we called the green zone. This was an ideal area for insurgents to hide. That is where we took most of our fire from. We took a mounted patrol out into the desert area because there are some villages there and we were trying to regain some of the support we had lost. While we were there, we got a call from one of our guys who was watching the perimeter on the cameras we had set up. He notified us that there was no one at guard point ten. I told him to send someone out on a four wheeler to check the perimeter and other guard posts, because the team before us said that they had all of their ANA (afghan national army) just leave in the middle of the night, taking their weapons, ammo, NODS, and radios, and defect to the Taliban. That was one of the first relationships we tried to mend when we brought in a fresh batch of Afghan guards. That was important because they guard our outer perimeter.

Our guy notified us that all of the guard positions, but one, were unguarded. The Afghans had left. The only ones who stayed were six soldiers from Tajikistan which borders northern Afghanistan. We then cut short the patrol we were on and we headed back to the firebase. So now, we have our ten-man team, five ANA that are pretty much useless because they are new, and we have to start pulling security as we're building infrastructure.

On the 16th of August, I was in the operations center and my guys were coming in for lunch, when all of a sudden we heard a big boom. This is nothing new because occasionally the Taliban would fire an RPG towards the camp. There were about six of us and my guys went outside to where the tower was to try to get a view of what was happening. I was watching the cameras in the ops center and I noticed one of them was completely clouded out, and it is guard point ten. We started to put on our kits and as I was watching the camera, the dust was settling, and I saw two insurgents trying to pull a third guy away from guard point ten. The Marines had sent out a construction crew to build us a berm and after they made the berm, we would string concertina wire. Guard post ten was not finished yet.

I decide to go out there on a vehicle with a marine dog team and a metal detector. We got out there and detected another IED, so we blew that one in place. That was two IEDs in that spot, so I figured they were targeting the Marine crew. So, they couldn't finish the berm in that spot. We went into the guard point, and it's just a built up area with sandbags on three sides and a plywood cover on top.

My team was following the blood trail which went around behind the position, and down the embankment outside the perimeter toward the green zone. Between us and the green zone is a road. A couple of my guys were looking through sniper scopes trying to see any activity in the green zone. I told my guys

I wanted a vehicle to go out with a dog and metal detectors to see if the blood trail went into the green zone. I had other guys get into an MRAP (mine resistant ambush protected) vehicle, which has better optics and watch the other vehicle going out.

My buddy, Mark, was standing next to me and turned to take a step and set off an IED. I remember staggering back and saying, "Oh no, not again." It didn't blow me off my feet, but I was thinking I probably should sit down. I laid back and I could hear the guys; they came over and started working on me. I was aware of them putting tourniquets on my left arm and both of my legs. I couldn't open my eyes due to shrapnel injuries. The enemy started firing in our direction, but it wasn't very effective. My guys were calling for a medevac but there was some confusion because medevac wouldn't come in unless the area was secured.

I can remember yelling, "Just clear the fucking LZ (landing zone) for the medevac." When I said that, I could feel the right side of my mouth flapping, so then I knew I had facial injuries. I could feel the blood from my nose because the explosion blew the tip of my nose off. Mark said he could see me and told me my left arm looked badly damaged and my face was bleeding a lot. I also had a chunk of wood, about a foot long and three inches around, stuck in my leg. I had a femoral cut on my right leg. I had a pretty severe wound to my stomach, just below my body armor. All of my injuries were to my front. Mark lost his left leg to the hip and his right leg above the knee. He also lost his thumb on his right hand and part of his middle finger on his left hand.

Finally, a British medevac helicopter came in to get us. They loaded Mark into the bird first, then I was put onboard. Once my stretcher hit the floor of the chopper, I lost consciousness. From what I have been able to piece together, we were flown to Camp Bastion which is a Marine base in Helmund Province. We were transferred to another aircraft and flown to Bahgram. They kept us there over night and the next day we flew out to Landstuhl, Germany. We stayed a few days there and then I was transported to Walter Reed Army Hospital, arriving on 21 August, 2010. My buddy Mark was also sent to Walter Reed and he and I are now at Bethesda Walter Reed Hospital.

When I arrived there I still had my left arm; however, it looked as if it had been deboned, it was a mess. The doctors tried to save my arm. They took an artery out of my leg and grafted it to my arm; but one night the artery blew, and there was blood everywhere, even on the ceiling. Ultimately, they had to remove my arm. I had quite a bit of endochondral ossification where my bone just started growing back to where it felt like a log.

I spent three months in hospital because of that. In June of 2011, I had an operation to remove the excess bone that had grown. Through all of this, I basically started relying on my right hand; however, I had lost my forefinger and had limited use of my middle finger. I've got bone on bone and tendon damage going on with my hand. The only thing I've got working fully is my thumb.

I've had a prosthetic for around nine months now, but I don't use it very much because I've gotten used to using my right hand, even though it's only at about forty percent. I'm also a bit self conscious about wearing my prosthetic, so that's part of the problem.

I had my eyes sewn closed for six weeks because of the shrapnel injuries to them. The problem with that is, they had put me on Ketamine, a drug that causes a person to have hallucinations, and I was convinced that I was blind. It made it very hard for me to differentiate between what was real and what was not. I had some pretty strange dreams, one of which was that I had my family on a camping trip in Afghanistan. I thought the nurses were trying to kill me. Believe me, it was not a pleasant experience at all. As of now, my right eye is back to 20/20, and I have partial sight loss in my left eye in the lower left quadrant, which makes my vision a bit foggy.

My second Purple Heart was presented to me by Colonel Bolduc, my old battalion commander, at Walter Reed. He had come down to Firebase Robinson just the day before the IED explosion. I was asking for a lot of support so he personally came to our firebase to look things over and we walked around that some area near guard post 10.

I have a job waiting for me back in 3rd Group, if I choose. I have wrestled with that idea because the two IEDs and my time spent at Walter Reed have really done a number on my family. I mean, it's really been tough. So, I'm looking at retiring right now. I have been in the military for twenty-one years and have attained the rank of Master Sergeant. I've had a great career. I've been able to do all the things I've wanted to do and really enjoyed it. Had that second IED incident not happened, I would still be there because I was planning on staying for thirty years. That was my passion, and it was taken from me. So now I have to find that one thing that will get me up at four o'clock in the morning and be excited to go to work. I've had a couple of ideas but nothing that made me say, "Wow."

I grew up in a Christian home and those values were instilled in me all my life. I have been slapped in the face with the realization that on two or three occasions I should have died. With that in mind, I am sure that God has something else for me to do. I don't know what it is, but I have to believe that. So, I'll just have to wait and see what it is. There is a wonderful woman who works here. She's like a little angel who has been able to get me and Mark interested in attending Georgetown. One of my interests these last few years has been going out and getting a college degree because I left for the Army right out of high school. Perhaps in doing that I will find that one thing that gets me up, once again, at four o'clock in the morning.

My old sergeant major, who I served with in Germany, had done some crazy ass things in his career. He had been involved in Korea, Panama, and Mogadishu, and was one of the best NCOs I've ever met. He had this saying, "Be careful what you wish for, because you just might get it." Using that train of thought, I will say that war is a dirty, nasty, ugly thing. Before we ever commit one U.S. soldier to a combat environment, we need to make sure we've tried everything else; and after that, if we need to commit, you send that soldier, along with the kitchen sink, and you have him fight it dirty, nasty, ugly, and as quickly as you can to win it. Anytime you tip toe through a situation and try to tread delicately, you automatically increase the number of casualties. War should be avoided at all costs, but I don't think the war in Afghanistan could have been avoided. It's something that had to be done. Not because the Taliban attacked us, but because they allowed terrorism to flourish in their country and allowed terrorists to train there to bring the fight to us.

I also believe the war in Iraq was necessary because the world is a much better place with Saddam Hussein gone. Democracy in Iraq, regardless of the form it takes, is a good thing for its people, and for the rest of the world.

12

YA' GOTTA STOP
SARGE, REALLY

My name is Patrick Percefull and I am from Fort Worth, Texas. I am a Staff Sergeant in the United States Army. I joined the military on 30 May, 2002 mainly because of 9/11. Our country was going to war and I wanted to be a part of that.

I did my basic and advanced training at Fort Benning, Georgia. After completing that I was sent to the 3rd Infantry Division, Fort Stewart, Georgia. I did two combat tours with 3rd ID, and in between those deployments I took my airborne training.

My first deployment was during the initial invasion of Iraq. My unit advanced from Kuwait, into Iraq and all the way up to Baghdad. We hit Najaf, Al Nasharia, Karbala, Karbala Gap, and eventually the airport at Baghdad. I spent about twelve months in Iraq.

Upon my return to the states, I went to Ft. Benning and attended jump school. Upon the completion of jump school and acquiring my jump wings, I went back to the 3rd Infantry Division. In 2005, I again deployed with 3rd ID to Northern Iraq, near Mosul. That deployment lasted another twelve months.

I came back to the states and got a job as a recruiter in Boston for three and a half years. After that, I went to Germany for a year with the 2nd Cavalry Regiment. I left there to go to selection for Special Forces. After being selected, I went to the "Q" course at Camp Mackall, where I went through language school and patrolling, but I ended up hurting my back during the patrolling phase. So, from there I ended up in the 82nd Airborne Division. I was assigned to 1/504th Delta Company. I deployed with the 504th to Afghanistan in the RC East Region, Ghazi Province, at FOB (forward operations base) Morqur.

Operation No Leaf Clover began on May 22nd, 2012 as a two-part operation to be conducted over a two-day period. We were to air assault into a town called Alam Kehl, where, on the southeast portion of the town there was a known explosives factory. Our mission was to destroy the explosives factory and then, in the morning, patrol through Alam Kehl looking for enemy bed-down sites.

The first part of the mission went flawlessly. We air assaulted in on Chinooks at three in the morning in the pitch black. We had a full platoon. We also had a large number of ANA forces with us and that can sometimes be tricky, but they did their jobs well. We hit the explosives factory without any opposition before the enemy could put up a fight. We found 250 pounds of explosives, plus all the equipment necessary to build bombs. This factory was basically making the explosives that then went into containers for making IEDs. We blew up the factory and spent the night there.

The next morning we headed out through Alam Kehl,

looking for the enemy and found them around 10:00 am. Whether they were waiting for us or we caught them with their pants down, I don't know, but we ran into about a dozen Taliban. They were located in an isolated qalat, about twenty feet by twenty feet with mud walls, which was located in a wheat field.

The Taliban initiated fire when we were about two hundred meters out. We hit the dirt and started to return fire. I grabbed my squad and headed over to a grape vineyard. The way the vineyards are cut, they make natural trenches which provide good cover. I had my alpha team maneuver around to their flank. Now there is nowhere for the enemy to run. We had our M240B machine guns in place, Saws (squad automatic weapons), grenade launchers, and the fight was most definitely in our favor. The vineyard gave us excellent cover and concealment.

The Taliban decided to launch their RPGs into the air as you would a mortar round. Out of the five or six that they fired, one got lucky and it landed right next to me, about a foot and a half to my right front. Pieces of shrapnel hit me in the neck and shoulder. Sergeant Welcheck was hit in the right knee and Specialist Harris was hit in the left shoulder. I was hit pretty bad and I saw my right arm flop on the ground, and it was completely numb. I picked it up and shoved it in my gear, thinking it had been blown off. At the time, I didn't know I had been hit in the neck. I picked up my rifle with my left hand and displaced over to get on the radio and started getting a casualty assessment from the team that was with me. I was calling up on my radio and Sergeant Welcheck came over and said, "Hey,

Sarge, you gotta stop, you really gotta stop and lay back."

I said, "Yeah, I know; I'm hit in the shoulder."

He continued with, "Ya gotta stop, Sarge, really." At that point Private Wells, our platoon medic, came over and I had no idea what he was doing; but, he messed with it awhile and I found out that some of the shrapnel had ended up in my neck and severed my carotid artery. Later on some of the guys were telling me they actually saw the exposed artery and it was squirting out blood. I don't know how Private Wells kept me alive, and conscious, but he did. He sure knew his business. All this time I had a genius in my platoon and never knew it.

By the time the helicopters arrived I was able to walk over to where they were. It didn't take long for them to get there because we had two attack helicopters and a Blackhawk on station. I went out on the Blackhawk to FOB Warrior, and immediately transferred to Bahgram Air Base and from there to Landstuhl, Germany. I arrived at Bethesda Walter Reed Hospital on 25 May, 2012.

Initially, I got to the point where I could move my right arm, but had limited motion. My hand was still paralyzed, and I had quite a bit of nerve pain in my arm. I've had four operations on my neck. At this time I am able to grip with my hand and hold a pen and write my name. I will be heading back to Ft. Bragg in the very near future to rejoin my unit. They have all the facilities and equipment that I will need for my physical therapy.

My Purple Heart was presented to me by a British General named William C. Maryville in charge of RC East, at Bahgram.

He told me a story while he was presenting me with the medal and said that the Purple Heart originated during the Revolutionary War and was presented to three American soldiers for the capture of a British Major, John Andre. The original award was known as the Fidelity Medallion, to later become the Purple Heart. So, a British General was now presenting a Purple Heart to an American soldier, which we found rather amusing.

I plan on going back to Bragg, continue my Army career, and retire from the military. I'm having some trouble with my trigger finger so I may have to learn to shoot left-handed.

My view on the war is that, as long as we're fighting them over there, we're not fighting them here. There are a lot of Americans who just don't understand that. They're always saying we should bring the troops home, but they don't see the big picture. Since the War on Terrorism, we haven't had a significant attack here in the United States. I'm sure there have been some planned that have been stopped before they had a chance to carry them out. The actual intelligence that we are finding over there is priceless. Every soldier they train, every dime they spend, every RPG they fire over there, are resources they can't use on us here. I do feel very strongly about what we are doing over there and we very much need to be there.

13

ZHARI DISTRICT, KANDAHAR PROVINCE

Hi, my name is Wyatt Harris and I am originally from Spanish Fork, Utah. I joined the U.S. Army in February of 2009 after graduating from high school. I joined because I wanted to make something of my life, and, as a little boy, I always dreamed of being a soldier. I left for Fort Knox, Kentucky on February 18, 2009 for my basic training. After completing basic, I went to Fort Sill, Oklahoma where I attended advanced individual training to become a Fire Support Specialist, commonly known as a FISTR. Upon completion of AIT, I was assigned to 4th Squadron, 4th Cavalry Regiment at Ft. Campbell. In February of 2011, I deployed to the Zhari District, Kandahar Province, in southern Afghanistan.

In September, my troop was assigned the mission of building a new outpost for the ANP (Afghan National Police). The area was secured by my troop and a support unit was brought in to clear the area and set up concrete barriers around a set of conexes (large metal storage containers). Upon completion of the support unit's mission, both platoons of my troop collapsed back to the new outpost. In order to maintain hygiene and morale, our two platoons rotated back and forth between the

ANP outpost and our own Troop Combat Outpost. The only thing left to do was to bring the men of the ANP outpost in and the mission would be complete. For unknown reasons, these guys had yet to be seen, which left us manning their outpost. We took sporadic small arms fire combined with 82mm recoilless rifle and RPG fire throughout our stay, at what became known as the PPS site.

On October 8, my platoon leader's truck was struck by an 82mm round on the passenger side window area, severely wounding my platoon leader (Lt. Scribner), sending shrapnel into the gunner's leg (Specialist Smith), and causing a TBI (traumatic brain injury) to the dismount (PFC O'Connor). At the time, I was sitting about fifteen feet to the rear of the vehicle and was struck on the right side by shrapnel. I was hit in the thigh and just under my armpit. As a platoon, we had plenty of experience at engaging the enemy, and we did just that. My job requires me to work with artillery, mortars, and all sorts of aviation assets. While wounded, I began coordinating with an Apache gunship and a Kiowa Warrior chopper, to engage the area where contact with the enemy was made. I knew I was wounded, but I had seen Lt. Scribner's wounds and knew the enemy had to be engaged in order to land a medevac chopper. After the first gun run from the Kiowa, I informed my platoon sergeant (SFC Macey), that I was wounded and began receiving treatment from my buddy (Sergeant Johnson). A tourniquet was applied to my leg and a pressure dressing was wrapped around my chest. The medevac bird checked in with me and I instructed them where to land. A group of eleven soldiers, including the wounded, moved out to the evac site. Smith, O'Connor and I helped each other onto the Blackhawk and we were soon airborne.

The ride to Kandahar was about fifteen minutes, which gave the flight medic time to cut my pants up to the wound area and loosen the tourniquet. When we landed, all kinds of medical personnel took us in for treatment. My clothes were immediately cut off and I was stuck with needles containing some kind of medicines. X-Rays were taken of my side which revealed the shrapnel in my armpit was just under the surface of my skin. The doctor cut the entrance wound to the site and removed the piece of metal. The staff checked me over quite well, bandaged me up, and sent me to the wounded warrior barracks.

Back at the PPS outpost, the platoons were swapped and the mission resumed. I was sent back to my platoon about a week later and continued on with the deployment. After returning stateside, I've been seen a couple of times to have the shrapnel in my leg removed. Sometimes I have trouble hearing from my right side. I've started to show signs of TBI that I feel I need to be treated for. Currently, I am still stationed at Ft. Campbell. To this day I have not had a proper ceremony for my awards, although it is listed on my personnel records.

The nice thing about Afghanistan was when you were able to see the people taking care of themselves. There were times when it actually happened.

I am planning on going to helicopter flight school and becoming a Warrant Officer or finishing my existing military time and going to college.

14

You're the Best
Damn Squad Leader
I Ever Had

My name is Christian Brown and I'm originally from Memphis, Tennessee. I am a Corporal in the United States Marine Corps. I joined the military in August, 2009. I realized all the freedoms and liberties that I had and felt a heavy weight on my heart that I needed to contribute to the cause. Inwardly, I always felt that I wanted to join the military and that I would be good at it. I was.

I did my boot camp at Parris Island, South Carolina and my advanced training was at Camp Geiger, North Carolina which was infantry training. I was then sent to the fleet and stationed at Camp Lejeune, North Carolina. I was assigned to 1st Battalion, 6th Marines.

My first deployment was in 2009, to Marjah, Afghanistan and we were the first boots on the ground there. While there, I was assigned as a gunner on a MATV, an up armored hybrid of the Hummer. I was a turret gunner and operated a few different systems to include the Mark 19 (grenade launcher), M240, and the M2 .50 caliber, often referred to as Ma Deuce.

My first deployment lasted seven months, after which I returned to the states at Camp Lejeune. I went home and did some visiting with family and friends and then, upon my return to Camp Lejeune, my unit started to do a work up for our next deployment. We did a lot of training in different places to get ready.

My second deployment was in August, 2011 to Sangin, Afghanistan. Initially we reported to Camp Leatherneck and we were to relieve 1st Battalion, 5th Marines out of Camp Pendleton, California. From there we went out to a PB (patrol base) named Transformers, which was already established, and we stayed there for about two or three months. During that time we were shown how to do patrols by the guys who had been there before us. There wasn't much going on there.

Word came down that there was a big operation coming up. It had to do with Kajaki Dam and restoring the power there. The Taliban had taken control of it and broken it down. My battalion was airlifted to the north of the dam and established Whitehouse. I was not part of that, my battalion was; however, I was sent across the Helmund River to a place called Black Rock. Our company was delivered there by an Osprey and we were basically cut off from the rest of battalion. Most of the fire battalion was receiving was coming from across the river, so that is why we were over there, to find and silence the enemy. The place where we set up was named PB Manassas. We were about three clicks (three thousand meters) away from Whitehouse, so if we needed support, we could get it quickly by helo.

After establishing our base, we immediately sent out patrols to see what we were up against, checking for IEDs and making sure the perimeter was safe. We were expecting contact, and within twenty-four hours it happened. We were in a firefight. Corporal Hohl had the patrol out and he was the one who initiated contact. That was within 5200 meters, so basically we walked right out our front door and had contact with the enemy.

As we were receiving small arms fire, we were also catching IDF (indirect fire) from Russian made mortars, 30mm grenade launchers, and more. After that firefight, we proceeded towards a village, set in a valley between two mountains, the Helmund Valley. The enemy had spotters who already knew how many we were, where we were going, and such. We attempted to counter that by utilizing some high ground we called Stonewall. We split into two teams of six men each, one team on the mountainside, and the other to enter the village.

Within the first forty-eight hours we found and destroyed three large enemy bunkers set up to rain fire down upon Whitehouse. They were well built with dirt pushed up against them and fortified with logs. As we blew those positions in place, we started receiving fire from secondary positions the enemy had.

I was a Lance Corporal and a squad leader and had a sergeant over me, so I was basically learning a lot of this as I went along. But, it was good to know I had someone to rely on if I had to ask questions. I pushed the guys a lot and I was pretty aggressive, but they liked that about me.

There was a Marine in my squad by the name of Lance Corporal Leavy who was of Native American descent, from the Lumbee tribe. He was a combat replacement, which means he had returned from a deployment in Afghanistan and asked to be sent right back. So he became part of my team. I got to pick who I wanted and I picked Leavy because he looked squared away, seemed sharp and attentive, went to some schools, and was organized, so that was why I wanted him. I believe he was nineteen years old and I watched him operate. One day I sat one of my team leaders down and told him that Leavy was taking over his team. He was assigned as a DM (designated marksman), so he got the scoped rifle with a silencer. He was my eyes and ears as to what was going on around us; he was my go to guy. He had already taken out a few of the insurgents.

On this patrol, we pushed through to the south side of the city, and we made ourselves a good foothold. Suddenly, the building we occupied started taking fire. I sent Leavy and two other Marines to the roof to be our eyes and ears as to what was going on around us. I learned from our spotters that we were receiving fire from three different locations. We were involved in what was called a complex ambush. My interpreter had a radio that scanned all the Taliban frequencies and he could listen in and let me know where the fire was coming from.

I called back to Manassas for air support, and in the meantime we started receiving heavy indirect fire from the enemy tubes (mortars). I contacted my team leader, Lance Corporal Harding, and told him to maneuver his team around the building as we established what was going on from the rooftop. Around this time, Lance Corporal Leavy was on the rooftop and caught a round to his head. The round entered his left temple and the Kevlar helmet caused the round to change direction and continue on to the back of his skull. I ordered my Marines off the roof and Leavy made sure the junior Marines with him made it down first before following them.

As Leavy got down, I was right there. As he went limp, I immediately cradled him in my arms. Doc was right behind me and started to assess Leavy's injury. I took Leavy's hand and said, "Hey Lord, I'm in a situation I can't control. I need your help to save this young man. I need you and the Holy Spirit to do things I can't do."

As I released his hand I called for the bird to come in and gave them the nine line. It includes all the information that bird needs to know about the casualty, what equipment they need to bring, where the landing zone will be established according to grids, who's calling in the bird, and the casualty's vitals.

We removed Leavy's helmet and Doc wrapped his head with a pressure bandage, but he was bleeding really bad. The inside of his helmet was full of blood and what looked like brain matter. I knew this Marine was really bad off so when I called for the medevac, I said, "Urgent, Urgent." That lets any air traffic in the area know I have a priority case. I was talking to Leavy trying to keep him from going into shock. His body was starting to seize up and I told him if he could hear me to squeeze my hand, and he did.

I needed to find a clear area for the bird. The only problem was that all the buildings in the area are interlocked, and as we started to move, we received fire and were pinned down. We tried breaking through the mud walls to make an escape path. Finally, I said, "We just gotta fuckin' move." Some of the other

Marines were having a hard time with this because when Leavy got to the squad he became a buddy to everyone; he just fit right in.

I, and two other Marines, went out the door and started laying down fire so the other guys could move Leavy toward the LZ. We finally reached the LZ and popped red smoke for the bird to land. I told my men to form a line and as the bird came in we started laying down fire to keep the enemy's heads down. As the bird was coming in all looked good, but the bird waved off. I told my guys to cease fire and change out their magazines. I got notification that the bird was coming back in, so I popped smoke once again. The area that the bird had to land was small, but a savvy pilot could do it, and I was hoping they realized the severity of the situation.

The bird came in again over my shoulder and I nodded at the pilot; he nodded back, and as it got about fifteen feet from the ground, it waved off once more. At this time, Doc says, "He ain't gonna make it; he ain't gonna make it."

I radioed back, "Leavy is not on the bird. I repeat, Leavy is not on the bird."

At that time, my Staff Sergeant told me, "You're gonna have to take Leavy to the south side of the city." What I didn't know at the time was that the area the bird had to land in was a courtyard with about a two-foot wall on one side. As the chopper came down the rotor blades were bowing and would have clipped the wall, and we would have had more casualties.

We moved out about one hundred yards to a spot that looked good for the medevac, and as we got there the bird was already landing on its own. I had no more smoke to pop, I was out. The problem now was that between us and the bird there was about a twelve-foot gully. I was concerned we might injure Leavy more or another guy would hurt himself, so I waved the bird off and we retreated back into a building. By now, I had Marines starting to panic; they were bone tired, basically wasted. I knew I had to make a decision, so I threw my rifle to one of the guys and picked up Leavy, put him on my shoulders, and started running to the south side of the city.

At this point I was operating on pure instinct. All I knew was that I had to get this casualty to the bird. I kept talking to Leavy and telling him he was gonna be alright, but I could feel his body getting limp. I ran for about five hundred meters, then I went down on my knees; they felt like they were on fire, and I couldn't catch my breath. I looked up and I saw the bird and the pilot motioned to me that he was coming down. I heard boots behind me and my guys took Leavy from me and loaded him on the chopper. We finally received air support and they started hammering the positions where we were taking fire from. They then followed us all the way back to the PB.

We got back to the PB and I've always been a strong guy. At the time I was 220 pounds, 6 feet, 1 inch, so, you know I was a pretty big dude. I was good at holding back my emotions, but we had to carry all of Leavy's gear back and that will play on your emotions. It's like you've just stripped someone of his identity, because that person has been with that stuff every day. That's his shit and you hate taking it. Some of the guys were just balling as they put Leavy on the bird, and I had been holding back. I had some anger, frustration, emotions, and I just couldn't talk because I was afraid if I did I'd burst into tears too. It was like swallowing an apple.

I let my team leaders orchestrate the route back to the PB. Upon arrival I immediately went to the COC, our command center, and I broke down in front of my Lieutenant, my platoon sergeant, and I just cried and threw my Kevlar because I was so angry, so angry because I had planned this patrol so thoroughly and thought I had everything just right. Now I felt ashamed and I was thinking that nobody would want to go out again with me.

Word filtered down from Whitehouse that Leavy was alive when we loaded him on the chopper. They said, "Leavy ain't doin' too fuckin' good, but he ain't doin' no worse. You got him on the fuckin' bird, you did your job. He's okay right now." That gave us all some relief. Unfortunately, Lance Corporal Leavy did not make it; he died a few days later.

I went to my platoon sergeant and told him that my guys needed a break because of all the time we'd been there. That was the most substantial firefight we had been in. My platoon sergeant replied that they can't take a break, because there was a company-wide effort taking place and there were three squads undermanned. I had to go back to my squad and tell them that if we didn't go out the next day, maybe another one of our buddies gets hurt.

I was really concerned for my guys. I knew that every time we went out the gate, anything that might go wrong was on my shoulders. It was a heavy burden to carry so I wanted to be sure I was up in the front of the squad, that way, if anything happened, I'd be the first to see it or the first one to hit it. Now, I've had some close calls in previous firefights. I caught a round under my armpit and it went up and through my pack, ruining everything in it. Another time I was peeking around the corner of a building and a round hit near me, showering my face with debris.

On this particular day, 13 December, 2011, our Lieutenant was going along, and he told me what he wanted done. So, I planned the route and all the other things that go along with the mission and he seemed okay with it. The drones had seen the enemy in a certain area and we were going out to get those assholes. Our Lieutenant knew that if anything needed to be done, I was his go-to guy; we had a good rapport. Right after the Leavy incident, General Craparotta came and meritoriously promoted me from Lance Corporal to Corporal.

We pushed halfway through the city without being seen. We knew that because there was no traffic on the ICOM, the enemy radio. I pushed into a building and told the squad leaders that they got it. I let the Lieutenant know what we were about to do and he was fine with it. I had two guys on the corner of one building and two more on the corner of another, so they could watch our front. I exited the building, taking a right step, and within ten meters, I hit an IED.

When this happened, everyone thought we'd taken indirect fire, except for the two guys on the corner of the building who saw it happen. I flew about eight feet into the air, did a complete flip, and landed on my back, sprawled out. The strap on my

Kevlar helmet snapped and it flew off my head. I thought, Oh, shit. I knew I'd been hit, and for a few moments it was like my mind and body were trying to catch up with each other.

Even though my ears were ringing, I could hear someone yelling, "Oh shit, oh shit, he's hit, he's hit." That was my confirmation that I was indeed hit, hearing someone else saying it. I was trying to reach for tourniquets but I had trouble getting up; the reason being that my pelvis was blown open at the front like an open book.

My best buddy Harding was right there telling me, "I gottcha brother, I gottcha," so I knew I was being taken care of. Then I raised both my arms to do an assessment and they looked okay. However, because I had on my gloves, I didn't know at the time that I had a finger that I was going to lose. So, I'm thinking, I'm okay, I still got something left.

They cordoned off the area and started to lay down fire, as my Lieutenant called for the bird. As that happened I was asking my buddy Harding if I had my legs and he was saying, "Whatcha all fuckin' worried about that for man, I gotcha; you're about to get three hot meals a day, sleepin' on a cot, you're starting to piss me off." He was talking to me the way he knew I needed to hear it.

My Lieutenant came out and when he saw me, he just broke into tears, because I was one of his favorites. He was standing over me saying, "You're the best damn squad leader I ever had; you're a golden boy. I want you to know that I'm damn proud of you Brown. Then my buddy Harding even started to cry.

They put me on a litter and carried me out to where the

bird was coming in, and as they did, I reached over and grabbed Harding's wrist and told him, "Hey buddy, I love you." I asked him again if I had my legs, and by his responses and the way he kept trying to keep my mind off the subject, I knew I had lost them. I just knew. By the way the younger guys were looking at me, I thought this was going to be the end for me, so I decided to make my peace with God. Instead of an existing prayer, I said, "Lord, I want you to know I did my best, and I put others before me."

They got me on the Blackhawk, and I was starting to slip in and out at this point. I asked one of the crewmen for a drink. Because I had lost so much fluid, I was thirsty. He told me okay, but only a little. Then they started an IV, and I didn't wake up until a month and a half later after being in an induced coma. From what I was told, I was flown out to Camp Leatherneck, then to Bastion, and from there to Bahgram, Landstuhl, and finally to Bethesda Walter Reed Hospital. I arrived there on 19 December 2011.

My lower left arm has a blast wound from the plastic that the HME was put into. It flew out and melted to my arm. A piece of shrapnel blew out my bicep. I'm missing my right index finger, my pelvis was damaged considerably, my left leg is gone just above the knee, my right leg is gone just about to my hip.

When they brought me out of the coma I was throwing tantrums. I thought I was still in Afghanistan because they had me on some pretty heavy duty stuff that had me hallucinating, Ketamine being one of them. I was given over one hundred units of blood.

My buddy Harding went back and picked my leg up, still with the camo and my boot on it. The area gets cleaned up so the Taliban can't use anything for propaganda purposes. It's also used for post blast analysis, so they can determine how the blast occurred, what was used, and the after effects of it. In this case I was informed that it was an eleven to fifteen pound jug of HME with a battery and pressure plate right on top, which is what I stepped on. They said if I wasn't as big as I was I would have died. I suppose I'm grateful that it wasn't one of my other guys, because I still think about Leavy and it weighs heavy on my heart.

My plans for the future are basically the same as the medical staff's, and that is to get me to the point where I'm comfortable functioning in society with my prosthetics, and to be able to cope with what I've got going on. I'm working on getting that Marine Corps drive back and making myself healthy again, so hopefully, I can remain in the Corps. I know I can't be an infantryman again; however, I can teach. I can be a mentor to new Marines.

I was awarded my Purple Heart by the Commandant of the Marine Corps, General James Amos. Even though I had a trach tube in and other lines I was hooked up to, and I was feeling a bit loopy, they had a barber come in and give me a high and tight haircut, and they ironed my blouse and helped me get into it for the presentation.

My feelings on the war are pretty much that we need to stay in Afghanistan because we are fighting a religion called muslim extremism, and as long as they are bringing their kids up the same way they were brought up, and lied to, and taught that killing us is the right thing to do, and that Allah will bless them, then there's always going to be that next generation of fighters. We need to be there to show the children that we are not the bad guy; we are there to help them, to change the next generation of Afghans.

15

I'm Not Losing Another One

My name is Kenneth Swartz and I am an HM3 Hospital Corpsman Third Class in the United States Navy. I am from Columbus Township, Michigan, near a small town called St. Clair. I joined the military in 2007 because I ran out of money for college and I knew I wanted to do something in the medical field, and I also wanted to do my part and join the military, so what better way than to join the Navy and become a corpsman.

Initially, I went to Great Lakes, Illinois where I did my boot camp. Upon completion of boot camp, I went across the street to Corps School. Then I was sent to Bethesda as a corpsman in the ICU from March, 2008 until March, 2010 where I learned quite a bit. I then took leave and went home before I left in April for California to begin field med training with the Marines for about two months.

From there I went to the CTM, Combat Trauma Management Course, for two weeks where I learned to work on real type battle casualties. While I was there, Chief Padilla came over and called out fifteen names, one of those was mine, and he told us we were being assigned to 3/5 Marines and would be leaving for 29 Palms, California to get ready to deploy in September. While there, I was involved in training exercises and getting to know the Marines and finding out what they expected of me. After that we all took leave and returned for the deployment in 25 September, 2010.

We deployed to Sangin Valley, Helmand District, Afghanistan. We got into Camp Leatherneck and spent about a week to two weeks before heading out to FOB (forward operating base) Increment in the Green Zone, the northern sector. I was with Kilo Company 3/5. I was originally there at FOB Increment, but a corpsman with 2nd Platoon got hit on a patrol so they sent me out to PB (Patrol Base) Fires to replace him.

On 14 October, 2010, we went out on a morning patrol and came back in without incident. They told us to get ready to go out on another patrol. Our 1st Platoon, 3rd Squad was out on patrol and they got lit up pretty bad. We were inside PB Fires and we could hear the firefight they were in. We got calls on the radio that they weren't taking any wounded, but they could not get fire superiority. They sent out 2/1, 2nd Platoon as a QRF (quick reaction force). Initially, we were supposed to go out and talk to some villagers but they had us waiting and waiting until we found out our mission had changed. We went out with some snipers and we were supposed to get around behind the enemy and as they were chased back the snipers could take them out.

Everything was good. We got out there and took cover in a compound, and our squad leader got this bad feeling that we may get cut off, so he told us to fall back and hook up with the platoon. As we headed back we cut across a few fields and came out at a compound and then all hell broke loose. There was shooting everywhere. I came around the corner of the compound and took cover. Lance Corporal Lopez came over and took a knee next to me and another Lance Corporal took to his knee on my other side and he looked shaken up. His face was pale and he was not responding verbally.

I slapped his face a few times to bring him around and just then there was this huge explosion. As it settled down, I listened for yelling and screaming for a corpsman, but nothing. Then Lance Corporal Lopez turned to me and said, "Hey, they're calling you up." That's when I jumped into a trench and took off in that direction, passing a sniper along the way who was watching out to our front. As I got to the end of the trench I saw Lance Corporal Catherwood lying in the water with three Marines holding him, and he appeared to be dead. The shooting had stopped so I went down and we removed his gear and I started CPR. I was not able to bring him around. He was gone.

We had been in a pretty fierce battle and sometime during it my squad leader was shot in the leg, so all he could do was crawl around calling in support on the radio. One of the snipers, Sergeant Abbate, took command and counterattacked through the mine field twice and cleared the way for the medevac to come in. His leadership made it possible for our guys to drive off the enemy. Had he not done what he did, I probably would not have made it out alive. Sergeant Abbate died a few months later on the battlefield and was awarded the Navy Cross posthumously. Lance Corporal Lopez would also die on the battlefield.

I heard someone yelling that another Marine was hit near the area where I first took cover, so I headed back along the trench thinking in my mind, "I'm not losing another one." I got into the ditch and I told myself to go out the way we initially came in. But I had to get to this guy quick, so I headed towards a three-foot cinderblock wall. At the end of it I started to make my way around the end and I stepped on an IED.

I was told it was a thirty pound jug of HME with a pressure plate and it blew a four foot hole in the ground. I was running pretty fast but a lot of shrapnel caught me in my stomach and bladder. It ripped me open and I had a lot of arterial bleeding, and my pelvis was ruptured. The blast threw me into the air and I was only out momentarily, but as I tried to open my eyes they burned from all the debris. Someone was taking my gear off and I tried to help, but I didn't realize my right hand was kind of messed up. My thumb was dislocated and the ligaments to my pinky were cut. My right lung was collapsed from the explosion.

I looked down at my legs and I could see my knees but my boots were gone and where I had my boots bloused there was shredded pants that were blood stained. I was thinking, I'm okay, I'm still good.

The guys put tourniquets on me and Corporal Delaney reached into my pocket and took out my morphine and I told him I couldn't have it because I was having trouble breathing and that would only slow my breathing and kill me. I never was in any kind of intense pain. I was the corpsman and I was trying to tell the guys what to do. I was starting to go in and out of consciousness because I was losing lots of blood and my blood pressure was so low.

The British helicopter landed and the guys loaded me on and I was having a tough time breathing and I said, "I can't breathe."

One of the British crewmen yelled, "We need a needle decompression, stat." The last thing I remember is thinking to myself, yeah, I called that one; I knew I needed that. Next thing I knew was I woke up in the ICU at Bethesda where I knew all the nurses, which was kind of weird, but also comforting at the time.

The route they took me on was from Camp Leatherneck, to Bastion, to Baghram, then on to Landstuhl, Germany where I spent a couple of days. On 19 October, I arrived at Bethesda. As bad as I was, I was up on my new legs in two months and I consider myself lucky.

I was awarded my Purple Heart by Admiral Robinson, Chief Surgeon of the Navy, while at Bethesda.

I feel we need to be in Afghanistan. The Taliban are ruthless, but there are many people over there who like us. We gave them support and they eventually started coming to us and giving us information. I was wounded early on, but the guys I talk to told me we did a lot of good in Sangin and it's a lot better now. It took a lot of lives and sacrifice to get that done, but then, most things in life don't come easy. It takes hard work.

I'll never forget Lopez, Abbate, and Catherwood. They paid the ultimate sacrifice and I was given a second chance. I took a lot of positives from that experience and plan on using them in the future.

I have no regrets joining the Navy. I knew full well what could happen. There's no reason to be pissed at the world about it. I lost both of my legs above the knees but that could have happened right here in the States in an automobile accident. If it had, I'm not sure I would have made it here. I was lucky it happened over there where everything I needed was immediately available. Plus, if it happened here, I wouldn't have the opportunities that I have been afforded because of the military. It is what it is. I mean, yeah, there are days when I wish I had my legs back, but I've gotten to a point where this is my life now. It's become quite normal actually and I'm comfortable with it. I'm even running now. I plan on going back to college, applying for med school, and becoming a doctor.

16

It's a Marlboro, Thank God

My name is John Carnes and I am a Corporal in the United States Marine Corps. I come from Los Angeles, California. I joined the military in August of 2009 because I needed to test myself and see if I was good enough to become one of the best. I had other family members who served. My Uncle Arthur was a Green Beret in Vietnam. It wasn't for that reason that I joined, or even for country, because when you get right down to it, and you're down range with bullets flying, people start getting killed, ideals and family only mean so much. I joined because I wanted that brotherhood that, no matter where I was or what was going down, they were there for me, and I for them. I found that in the Marines.

I went to Parris Island, South Carolina for boot camp and I was in 2nd Battalion, Golf Company. I was there from 31 August, 2009 until 31 November, 2009. After boot camp I went to SOI (school of infantry) at Camp Pendleton, California, assigned to Alpha Company. I was training as a reconnaissance Marine; however, with just five days left before completing the course, I broke my left ankle in three places. So, I was dropped from the reconnaissance course and was in recovery for about four months.

I was sent to the infantry and I was okay with that because they're the guys who kick in doors and do a lot of neat stuff. I was sent to 29 Palms, California, assigned to 3rd Battalion, 4th Marines, eventually ending up in India Company as a SAW (squad automatic weapon) gunner. This was a whole new beast. The Marine Corps Infantry does everything. I did land assaults, sea assaults, and a whole lot more. I spent about a year there.

My unit then deployed to Jordan in the beginning of 2011. We did some stuff there that I cannot discuss but it sure was neat. I returned to 29 Palms and went on leave in July. Upon my return from leave I was notified that we were going to Bridgeport in Northern California. We were headed for mountain warfare school in a cold climate. Afterwards, I found out that 3rd Battalion, 7th Marines, out of 29 Palms was headed to Sangin in the Helmand Province. They were looking for combat replacements and I volunteered. I was a Lance Corporal at this time. It was mid September of 2011.

Sangin, I found out, was one of the most deadly places in Afghanistan. Snipers were very active and it was an IED-infested area. In our thousand meter PB (patrol base), over two hundred IEDs were found. These were anti-personnel and anti-vehicle mines. The anti-personnel mines were meant to maim, not kill. The insurgents didn't want young men coming home in caskets. They wanted nineteen and twenty year olds coming back missing limbs. That had a much bigger psychological impact on the American public. Unfortunately, they were quite successful at it sometimes.

I was a team leader and requested to be switched to a different squad. My reason for that was because the squad leader and I did not see eye to eye, and I thought it a miracle that he didn't get someone killed. There were quite a few incidents where it certainly could have happened, and I was there to witness them. I told my superiors that I had to be put into another squad before something bad happened between me and this guy. I made up my mind that I wasn't going to die because of this guy, or lose any of my friends because of him. He was an idiot and I didn't want to see my brothers killed due to his actions. So, I asked the Staff Sergeant to put me in another squad.

Turns out that this particular squad leader kicked my bunk and said, "Get up, you're going out on patrol with us."

My reply was, "Hey, I'm not in your squad anymore."

He answered with, "I don't care, you're going out on patrol."

I said, "Fine."

I got all my gear on, went to the head, came back, and the guys said, "Oh, you're back?"

"Yeah, looks like I'm going out on this last patrol with you guys."

The Sergeant came by. "Hey guys, we're going here, we're gonna do this and this; Carnes is back with us, welcome back."

It was kind of a smart ass remark as he looked at me and smiled. I just had this look on my face that said, "I hate you, and I swear to God, I'm gonna kill you today."

He pulled me over to the side, since we'd had several confrontations in the past, and he said to me, "Listen, whatever we had, whatever beef we had back then, it's over now; we're good, me and you are good." He said he knew I didn't like him and whatever he did he was sorry. He said he wanted to patch things up.

I looked him squarely in the eye and said, "It's never gonna be fine. I'm never gonna like you, and I don't think you should be a Sergeant. In fact, I think you should be a PFC." He just looked at me, not saying a word, and the guys all looked at us, and I just walked away.

He didn't go out on patrol that day. Corporal McMillan took his place, for reasons unbeknownst to me. I'd like to think I had something to do with that. Anyway, we pushed out, heading east, southeast from the PB. We were headed to an area known as Quebec 3 Victor. This is where the majority of the IEDs were found and where most of our attacks came from.

There's a bowl, a valley out there that we didn't have eyes on; it was difficult to see. Our mission was to do a recon, find out where to put an outpost, sweep for IEDs, and RTB (return to base) before dark. On the way, we stopped at a house. I called it the Jersey Shore house because there was so much drama there. The guy who lived there would beat his kids, throw rocks at the girls, and he also had his son's family living there. And of course, Afghan women are just property so they got mistreated also. This was the only house in this first valley.

We were there, talking to them for about a half hour or so, and I had put the teams out for security, mine staying with Corporal McMillan. We left there and approached some saddlebacks, small rolling hills, and we got up on this one where we decided to build an outpost. We did a sweep for IEDs and found only some spent shell casings from previous firefights. We decided to go down and talk to some more of the locals, trying to ascertain what was going on around there. We were walking up a hill towards another hill that had earlier housed a compound that was blown up before I had arrived in country. I was told that a firefight had broken out there and after all the fighters inside had been killed, they found all the materials necessary for making IEDs. So, it was destroyed.

We proceeded down into a second, larger valley where there were more houses to the right and a large farm to the left side. The villagers here were a quiet people. We were walking along a goat path, knowing there were IEDs to our right, our left, and the path was well traveled. If we'd find something on our way we'd call it in and have EOD blow it in place, and then we'd continue on. I was third in the line, Corporal McMillan was in front of me, and Lance Corporal Putnam was the lead sweeper, and this kid was pretty damn good at finding IEDs.

We got about thirty meters down the hill and Putnam got a hit on an IED. We called it in and EOD showed up to our North. We were southeast about two hundred meters from the Patrol Base at this point. When we called the EOD team it was about 1100 hours and we had been patrolling since around 0630 hours, so we hadn't really moved that far; however, that was a decent pace in Sangin. Every patrol that went out had found something.

EOD left the PB in a truck and headed down what we called Rt. 66, which was basically a larger goat path that was just wide enough to accommodate a truck. They came to a stop at the edge of an old poppy field. Aguayo took Conny and two other guys and they swept through Quebec 3 Victor, popped up on the North side and linked up with the EOD team on Rt. 66. EOD swept back toward us, got to our position, and we showed them the IED. They dug it out of the ground. They then went back to their trucks, came back, and blew the IED. Then they found a three liter jug of HME, which had an anti-tamper switch attached to it, so that if it was moved or tilted, it would detonate.

The Taliban are low tech men in a high tech world. If you have a good man he can find the IEDs with little trouble. EOD blew this one in place and we witnessed a huge explosion, nothing new, and that was it. EOD headed out and we got ready to RTB (return to base). Aguayo had the radio. I had a THOR system, which is a unit that sends out a jamming signal to around thirty or forty feet. If we're near an IED and the insurgents try to send out a signal to detonate it, the THOR will jam the signal and not allow it to work. We got back to the trucks, gave them a wave off, and Aguayo got on the hook (radio) and sent back a message to the PB that we were RTB (returning to base).

We started moving out and we were walking on this path that people had been walking over multiple times. This had been stepped on over and over, so we thought we were good to go. We turned a little to the right to follow the same path. I was thinking to myself at this point, man, what would happen if I did step on a mine? Would I be okay? Would I be able to live a happy life missing both my legs? What happens if I lose my junk? There's a lot of stuff down there; what happens then? I'd just fuckin' shoot myself. Then I thought, Shit, what happens if I lose my hands? I'd have to have somebody shoot me.

All of a sudden I looked left while I was still walking, like a dumb ass, something we're not supposed to do. I should have stopped. All of a sudden I felt this intense, burning heat, while at the same time, all this dirt hit me squarely in the face. I didn't know it, but I was flying through the air at this time. I thought, oh shit, Conny's right in front of me. I did not just lose another of my friends, I did not, no!

Then, all of a sudden I hit the ground, and that's when I realized, I had stepped on it. I was the one. As I hit the ground, I screamed as loud as I could, "Oh, fuck, no."

I know everyone heard me, and all of a sudden I heard, "Whoa, what just happened?" I heard that and I didn't know who said it, but I said, "Are you kidding me; what the fuck do you think just happened?"

I looked and I saw Conny running towards me, and he was saying something, his mouth was moving, but I didn't hear anything. He got to me and put me on my back and then he was on the radio, "Carnes is hit, he's fucked up, both his legs are destroyed, we need help right now."

I didn't have a corpsman; my corpsman was across the valley with the rest of the patrol. They started sweeping and headed back towards us. While I was there, I took a look at my hands, touched each finger with my thumbs, moved my wrists, and checked out my arms. They were fine; I'm good. Then the moment of truth had arrived. Do I have my dick or not? I shoved my hand into my pants, I felt around and everything felt normal, I guess. I pulled my hand out, no blood.

Great, now what's wrong with my legs? My right leg was shattered below the knee and it looked like a big drumstick. The bone that connects it to the foot was showing, and my foot was gone. My foot was fragged into my left leg. My left leg was busted up below the knee and the lower part was turned completely around that my foot was in the cargo pocket of my pants. I picked my left leg up and I could still move my ankle. I thought, Cool, I can still move my ankle and my toes. It hurt, but, I could do it. I was thinking that was good, it was just broken. Then, all of a sudden, the blood started coming out, and I thought, Damn, I'm never gonna be able to drive stick shift anymore. I'm never gonna be able to drive my truck anymore. I had a 1996 Toyota Tacoma, a beautiful truck. It had a six-inch lift. I had the whole truck Rhino lined; my buddy did it. He sanded the entire truck and Rhino lined it. It was meant for muddin'. It really was cool.

So, what do I do if I meet a girl? What if I was a chick and some dude with no legs hits on me? I'd be like, What the fuck's wrong with you, get away from me. How would I ever be able to do these things again? I never thought I'd get laid because I got blown up. Turns out, you do.

At this point, Conny's freaking out. He said, "Carnes, you're gonna be okay, stay with me man."

This happened really fast and I was still wearing my Oakley sunglasses. Conny wanted to remove them and I told him he was not taking my sunglasses off. He told me he needed to look in my eyes. I said, "You can look in my eyes through the sunglasses. It's hot, the sun is really bright, I just got blown up, and I ain't taking them off!" Conny took them off and looked in my eyes. I said, "There, you saw my eyes, now put them back on. How do they look?"

Conny said, "Not too bad for a guy who just got blown up."

At this point we weren't getting shot at and I was thinking, "Damn, it's hard to breathe; why can't I breathe normally?" I took off my plate carrier. I undid the front of it and put it behind me and I laid on it.

Shit, I still can't breathe; maybe I'm at a weird angle. I pulled my camelback out and started drinking out of it. I still couldn't breathe right, so I thought, you just got blown up and adrenaline is pumping through your body. All of a sudden I realized, wait a minute, I can still feel everything down there.

I started moving my calf, moving my foot, and I could feel it moving, but, like my brain thought it was there, but it was not there, man. Then, all of a sudden, the pain came. Everyone says it's an excruciating pain, but it wasn't. It was more of a calming pain. It was this really deep, burning pain. It felt like someone just put my legs into a bucket of Tiger Balm, and it was this deep burning, soothing pain. I thought, getting blown up ain't all that bad.

I looked at Conny and he said, "Dude, you're gonna be fine, you're goin' home. You're finally gonna be able to sleep."

He put my tourniquets on and tended to my injuries and all of a sudden I said, "Man, I get to eat at Denny's for free for the rest of my life."

Conny looked at me and smiled and said, "Yeah, man, you're going to Denny's."

I started laughing and I laid back. Then all of a sudden it came. It hit me in waves, and I thought, you aren't fine; you just got your legs blown off, what the hell's wrong with you? Am I ever going surfing again, or snowboarding? How about back packing, or running? What about all that stuff? What about going to MARSOC (Marine Corps Special Operations Command)? That's my dream. I'm never gonna be able to do that now. That's all been taken away from me. I was about to be promoted to Corporal; I had a good thing going here, and now it's gone. Why the fuck, why, did this happen to me?"

The EOD trucks flipped it into reverse, came back, and picked me up. They had to have an escort with them, so my buddy Billy Elliot was in the rear vehicle. He came up to the truck and I said, "Yo, Billy."

He was like, "Oh, fuck." I could see that "oh shit" look on his face. He told them to sweep for secondaries because where there's one IED there's bound to be another.

At this point, I still had not been given any morphine. Billy came up to me and told them, "Let's get him on a litter."

I told them, "Hey, I can walk."

Then I looked at Conny and he said, "Nah, you ain't walking buddy."

I said, "Okay, fine."

So they put me on a litter and that hurt. They picked me up and it hurt my leg because I couldn't really control my ankle.

Finally, I was situated and I handed over my NVGs (night vision goggles), my weapon, an M4, my gear, compass, GPS, so that when I got back to the PB, I could turn over everything that was mine that has the serial numbers of the equipment I was issued.

O'Brien was in the turret and he turned around to help them get me into the MRAP truck, and my leg fell off the litter. I blurted out, "That's my fuckin' leg; get it."

He jumped down from the turret and grabbed my leg and said, "Dude, I'm so sorry man."

We had to go up this hill and I was strapped in the back of this truck. I had to put my hands on the back of the door and O'Brien said, "I got ya' man."

I tell him, "Get back in your turret and do your fuckin' job. Just let me lie here and be in pain."

As O'Brien was getting back to his turret, he turned around, looked at me and said, "You're a tough dude; you're tough."

I tell him, "Just get back in that turret and do your job."

We arrived at the PB and as they were unloading me, I noticed that everyone was there, I mean everyone. Anybody who wasn't on patrol was there. I had twenty guys helping me out of that truck. I felt like a king. They put me in the smoke pit so that I'd be away from the rotor wash of the choppers, and all the sand and dust that they kick up. The smoke pit is a designated area that's ringed with sandbags for us to go and smoke. Everybody on deployment smokes, mostly Marlboro. If you don't have Marlboros you smoke Pines (Afghan cigarettes) and they're disgusting.

So, I was in the smoke pit and Doc Lee came running up to me. Finally, I got a corpsman to check me out. He says, "Okay dude, you've got thermal burns and you're cauterized. You're not bleeding right now."

They ripped my pants open on my left and said, "Okay, your shit's broken."

"Really, you figured that out? I think I figured that out as soon as I got hit."

Doc says, "Okay, your left leg is broken, how bad I don't know. We'll see." He didn't take my boots off, he could feel my toes moving inside, and I could kind of move my ankle. Well, my foot got fragged and my big toe was cut. Doc said I had some bleeding in there, but I was good.

Doc Lee told me he was going to give me some morphine and I told him, "Okay, stick me, I've been waiting for this, stick me already." He stuck me and I waited. "I don't feel anything. You gotta be fucking kidding me."

Doc said, "Okay, I'll wait for fifteen minutes and stick you again."

I tell him, "Dude, you'd better stick me again right now or I swear I'm gonna kill you. C'mon, I need more, right now."

Doc told me, "Dude, you're a big guy, morphine's supposed to help; I mean, you're big."

I was a big guy. I was two hundred forty, and lifting the whole time I was in Afghanistan. I was huge. It took six guys to carry me, and that was without body armor on. That's why I set the damn thing off. I probably weighed close to four hundred pounds with all my gear on, plus my weapon.

Finally, after a second stick, I started to feel something, like a calming effect. Doc told me to drink some juice, that it would be good for me. It would put some sugars back into me, to help me from passing out.

"Fuck the juice; gimme some damn water." I drank most of the water in my camelback on the patrol, which was 120 ounces. I asked for a bottle of water and I chugged it down, then asked for a second one.

Gunny Martinez came up to me and I asked, "I guess I'm not going to MARSOC, Gunny?"

He was standing right above me and looking down and said, "Their loss, Carnes, because you'd make a damn fine MARSOC Marine."

So then I said, "Fuck you" to everybody. Some guy would ask how I was doing and I'd reply, "Fuck you, I'm fine."

All of a sudden my favorite sergeant in the whole world showed up and he started messing with my tourniquets, and Doc told him not to touch the tourniquets, and everyone's standing around talking and he starts to say something to Doc. I said, "Why don't you shut the fuck up? Just shut the fuck up right now. Who's missing a leg here? Who just got blown up? You got anything to talk about right now? No, you don't." I pointed right at him and said, "Get the fuck out of here right now or, so help me, I will kill you before I leave." I started to grab for a weapon and said, "Hell, I'll do it right now... Shit, my job's done, it's over. I can't do this anymore. If I'm able to kill just one more person, it's gonna be him." Finally, he left.

Now, I needed a cigarette and they gave me one. I looked

and saw that it was a Marlboro, thank God. As I was trying to light it, a chopper came down overhead and I had one hell of a time lighting my cigarette. Then I heard McMillan on the radio yelling, "No mother fucker, it's Carnes, Charlie, Alpha, Romeo, November, Echo, Sierra."

Apparently, they messed up my nine line to get me out. The only reason the bird was landing was because it was the Brits, and the Brits don't care. They're like, "Fuck that, dude's missing his legs and about to die. Get him on the bird and we'll deal with the other stuff later."

McMillan was trying to fix it; he saved my life. McMillan, Aguayo, Conny, and Doc Lee are the reason I'm here. Aguayo set up the medevac through our guys who fucked it up, and McMillan unfucked it with the assistance of the British. I was lucky the Brits had a chopper in that area at that time and they assisted. They had me out of there within fifteen minutes. They loaded me on the bird and everyone was there, except that one particular sergeant. Corporal Harms came up and yelled out, "I'll see you back at 29 Palms." Harms was a pretty cool guy, he was one of my friends over there. He was in my old squad, the one I wanted out of.

So, I'm on the bird and they're ripping my pants off and checking me out and this Brit says, "Right, you're missing below the knee, and your left leg is fucked up, but it looks like you're going keep it. You've got your cock and balls mate. You've got both your hands. Take a little vacation now; you're going to feel a little stick and prick."

My body was seizing up on me and then I just fell asleep.

They told me later that I died twice. The concussion caused a blood clot to form, collapsing both my lungs. This occurred at Camp Bastion, the British area there, in the trauma unit where the chopper had taken me. That's where they found out both my tibia and fibula were broken in my leg. I also had compartment syndrome, where the blood rushes to a certain area and has nowhere to go, so it causes my leg to expand. They had to open up my leg and do a fasciotomy, and had they not done that, I would have lost it, right below the knee. Thank God, I didn't experience any infection, which is what happens to a lot of guys with a similar injury.

For some reason, someone upstairs was looking out for me and didn't want me to lose any more than I already had. Looking back, I can say that is one of the best things that happened for me.

When I woke up, that's when I knew something was wrong. I was on a C-17 heading into Landstuhl, Germany. Some guy says to me, "Hey, you're Carnes, right?" I nod, and he says, "Your Dad's waiting for you."

What? My Dad? Here? What the hell was he doing here?

Something happened along the way for them to allow him to come here. The Marines made this happen. They got him a passport, a flight, and took care of the paperwork in under twelve hours. That's virtually impossible. They unloaded me and put me on a bus to take me to my room. I got in my room and I sat up, and my Dad said, "Wow, you're big."

I looked at him. "Hey, Dad."

All of a sudden I was out and flat lining with my Dad there.

Little did I know, I had a forty-eight hour window in which I was going to live or die. However, the odds were in my favor that I would make it. I was there for seventy-two hours. Within five days I was back in the states, at Bethesda Walter Reed.

They sent me to the Naval Medical Center in San Diego and while I was being treated there, I almost lost my leg. I was there for three weeks. So, they sent me back to Bethesda Walter Reed, where I've been ever since.

My right leg is a below-the-knee amputation, which is good. My left leg is pretty much completely healed and I can start running soon. I owe my left leg to Dr. Gordin who heard me say repeatedly that I wanted them to cut it off. Finally, he was able to say, "See, you guys are young and tuff, but I'm the brains of this outfit." Dr. Gordin was right. I love putting my pants on. You know most people take it for granted. Not me. To be able to stand up in the shower, to drive my truck and be able to shift. I don't have the beautiful Tacoma truck anymore, now I have a brand new Chevy Silverado with a crew cab and a pearl paint job.

Looking ahead, I plan on competing in the 2014 Para Olympic Winter Games for snowboarding. My plans include going to college and majoring in sports medicine. My real goal is to someday work at the State Department as a Diplomatic Security Agent. Those guys deploy all over the world and protect our diplomats, and on occasion, see some action. So, those are some of my goals.

At present, I'm seeing a very, very, very pretty young lady and waiting to see how serious that becomes. I'd also like to stay connected to this community because most people don't get to see this from the inside out. The guys who are just coming in need help, and it's a really big deal. It is for guys like me to say, "Hey, let's take care of you now." People always talk about the home of the free, because of the brave. They don't know that ninety percent of the people here are eighteen to twenty-three years old. Most can't even order a beer yet. I lost guys who were nineteen.

I lost a guy who was a virgin. Are you kidding me? Then I came home, and I was in New York City near the site of the 9/11 disaster, and I saw a guy holding a sign, 'Thank God for IEDs." I walked up to that individual and said, "Hey man, that's a pretty funny sign."

He said, "It's true."

So, I pulled up my pant legs and said, "If you only knew."

He looked at me and said, "Oh."

Then I said, "Why don't you put that sign down?"

He goes, "No, I believe in it."

I said, "You really believe in tearing families apart? Do you know how much pain and suffering is involved in that?"

Then he said, "Why are you over there killing babies?"

To which I replied, "I thought we left that in Viet Nam. Dude, you have no clue. How ignorant can you be?" I walked away.

A lot of people say being over there is a waste. My main job, besides taking out the garbage, was to improve life. We were doing the clearing, and doing some killing, but I was only taking out people who were trying to harm me and my friends. I was killing people who were harming innocent people. But, when I can go to a town and ask the villagers, "What can I do to make life better for you? You don't have to do anything for us." That's a good feeling. It's not a 'you scratch my back, I'll scratch yours situation'. You get to see a little town flourish, people growing things, kids actually getting an education, women doing things that they couldn't do before, other than be just an object. To see the kids playing games and not planting roadside bombs, that's great. People shouldn't say it's a waste unless they've been there, and bled, and unless they've seen how much good we're doing. Unless they've done that, then shut the fuck up, and let me do my job.

17

WILLIE AND ME

My name is Jonathan Grundy and I am a Sergeant First Class in the United States Army. I'm what is affectionately known as an Army Brat. I sort of grew up all over the place. However, I call Williamsburg, Virginia my hometown.

I joined the Army in May of 1995. I'm third generation Army. My grandfather was in for twenty years, serving with the old horse cavalry, and then under George Patton in World War II. My father served for twenty-eight years, seven as an enlisted soldier and twenty-one years as an officer. He retired in 1994.

Initially, I had planned on becoming an officer, but found out that I was ill prepared for college; so I decided to go back to Europe since I spent a lot of time growing up there. I enlisted with a guaranteed Germany contract. Originally, I wanted to go in for airborne infantry but you could not get a guaranteed European tour as airborne infantryman. My choice was as a cavalry scout.

I spent a year in Bosnia with the 3rd Infantry Division initially, and then there was a change to the 1st Infantry Division. We fell under the control of 1st Armored Division. We were only one cavalry squadron. I was there from December 1995 to December 1996. I then re-classed under the BEAR program, which is a shortage MOS program. I still wanted to be airborne infantry so I transferred to Fort Benning, Georgia and took basic training all over again. In January 1998 I graduated from jump school.

From there I ended up at Fort Bragg, North Carolina but did not become a member of the 82nd Airborne at that time. I volunteered for XVIII Airborne Corps LRRPS, which is long range reconnaissance patrol. I was put on a water team, but that didn't work out too well since I was a lousy swimmer; so, they put me on a mountain/desert team. I was on that team for a few years and then I went back to Germany once again as a cavalry scout. I knocked out a Macedonia, Kosovo rotation in the three years I spent there.

I then returned to Fort Bragg and had a guaranteed assignment with Alpha Troop, 1/17 Cavalry. At that time there was only one company sized element for the entire 82nd Airborne Division. With that unit, I did two tours of duty in Iraq. My first deployment was during the initial invasion of March, 2003. We operated in southern Iraq near Najaf, Al Samawah, Tallil, and we were there for about four or five months. Then I rotated back to the states. Within three months they wanted us to return to Iraq. This time would be for a significantly longer period, operating out of a base near Fallujah. We worked as far west as Jordan, as far north as Anaconda, and as far east as Bahgdad, just short of the Green Zone. I returned to Fort Bragg after that deployment.

At that time, they re-organized the entire 82nd with four brigades and put what I like to call a short squadron (a small cavalry squadron), consisting of a Headquarters troop, an Alpha and Bravo line troop, which are all scouts, and then a Charlie troop, which is all infantry. At that time I was assigned to 3rd Brigade with the 505th parachute infantry regiment, and we deployed to New Orleans, Louisiana to assist with the aftermath of Hurricane Katrina. We put the city under martial law and spent approximately thirty days there for what was called "Operation Helping Hand."

Upon my return to Fort Bragg, I was moved to 2nd Brigade 325th parachute infantry regiment, with 1/73rd Cavalry, Alpha troop. I deployed with them for my third Iraq tour in November of 2006. We were named Task Force Falcon and this time we fell under Special Operations Command, working out of Tikrit. This was only supposed to be a four-month deployment, but because we were doing such a good job, they extended us to six months. Then, they extended us for twelve, and then, sixteen months.

The vast majority of our missions were air assault by helicopters, courtesy of SOCOM; they had all the fun toys. For a battalion size mission we were allocated four Chinooks, with a standby chopper in case one broke down. We would have six Blackhawks and an additional one just in case. When 10th Mountain relieved my unit, their commander could not believe what we had available to us. It was unheard of for a battalion. We were averaging a minimum of one major mission each month.

My unit had been deployed for fifteen months. We were on day five of what was initially designed to be a three-day mission. We were doing so well at meeting our mission requirements that they kept us in there.

On one particular day, I was leading a patrol and we were just leaving an orchard, going into an area where there was a road, then a canal, a road, then another canal with some buildings on the other side. I had my guys in a staggered column formation with me as the point man. We came under fire from the buildings and, luckily, I was the only one hit. I took an AK47 round directly in the face.

As I fell backwards I got off three shots but I was momentarily knocked out. I was in a significant amount of shock. My mental process told me to breathe and I'd be okay. One of my Joes grabbed my body armor and pulled me behind a wall. My guys went into a defensive formation and started returning fire. However, the enemy was really good at hitting and running. They knew if they stuck around for very long, it was game over. We were gonna fix and finish them off.

Immediately we were on the radio with the PL, and some other platoons were flexed into the area. In the meantime, I was on the horn attempting to get some Apache helicopters into our area to locate and attack the enemy. An air medevac was sent out from Balad, which was not too far away, and the Blackhawk was there in about fifteen minutes. I couldn't walk, so they tried carrying me, and apparently I voiced my opinion to them in no uncertain terms that I would not be carried. So, I had a guy on either side, supporting me, helping me to the bird.

They loaded me onto the chopper and I was conscious the entire flight. I remember landing with medical staff meeting us at Balad. However, they must have hit me up with some heavy duty meds because from that point on all I remember is waking up with my jaw wired shut. They flew me out to Landstuhl, Germany where I spent three days, and then to Walter Reed Hospital. I arrived on the 14th of December, 2007.

I was immediately placed in the ICU and underwent eleven hours of surgery the next day for facial reconstruction and to repair the nerve. The round that hit me entered to the left of the bridge of my nose. It crushed my left nasal cavity, then tumbled, crushing the orbital core of my eye, and severing the facial nerve. It cracked my mandible in four spots then turned around and stopped. I cannot close my eye, so I wear a patch over it. They removed the bullet and I have it. The doctors were able to repair the facial nerve, and that's amazing, because it's like working with a fiber optic wire, very, very tiny. Then they sheathed it with a nerve piece from behind my ear. The doctors also cut behind my ear and peeled back my face to rebuild the crushed bone using a titanium mesh, then reattached my face. Over the years the bone has rebuilt itself around the titanium mesh.

The next surgery took five hours, and that was on my eye. When I awoke from that surgery, my dad was sitting there and broke the news to me that I would be blind in my left eye. My dad said that was one of the hardest things he ever had to do, giving me the bad news. It's been a bit tricky for me to get used to mono vision. Depth perception can be a tricky thing; you never think about it until something like this happens.

My jaw was wired shut for approximately three months and most of my meals were chicken and beef bouillon, Ensure, and Gatorade. The Red Cross supplied a really nice blender that we used to blend up different soups, but it got kind of messy, getting stuck in the wires. I ended up losing forty pounds.

Originally, I checked into what I had to do to stay on active duty. By that point in time, I had approximately twelve years in the Army. Once you reach that ten year mark, you might as well stick it out, especially if you love what you're doing. It's a good thing, and I love being a soldier. I had been on the list for E-7 Sergeant First Class and was promoted while I was in the hospital, and had my new rank pinned on me there. I had my Purple Heart pinned on me in theater; however, they had a representation ceremony at the 82nd Airborne Pre-Super Bowl Party in February of 2008 in the Malone House at Walter Reed. I was very weak at the time, having lost weight, and I was using a cane for support. My Purple Heart was presented to me by Colonel Bricker of the 82nd Airborne Division, and after the ceremony, which lasted about fifteen minutes, I went straight back to bed. I was exhausted.

So, I ended up fighting the system, finding out I was a no go on my medical evaluation board. I appealed it and that did me no good. My physical evaluation board came up, and I was no good on that too. I appealed it and was no good on that. You have an opportunity to have a case prepared for you with JAGs (Judge Advocate General) assistance, or prepare it yourself. I decided to have JAG assist me.

I started by stating my physical requirements, because I didn't want to change my job. My thinking was that I could go into a training environment or perhaps be a jump master instructor. My case was thrown out a day before the board convened because the president of the board, who was an infantry colonel, looked at the paper work and decided, "Yeah, this guy can stay in." I had a case prepared and was ready to show up in my dress uniform and say, "This is me; this is what I can offer the Army. Why get rid of me?"

Well, after that happened, I needed to find a job. I contacted my branch and they were not very helpful. Then I thought, maybe I could teach ROTC (reserve officer's training corps). I contacted cadet command for the eastern region and spoke to a Sergeant Major Green who was really squared away. He asked me what states I would be interested in, and I told him Virginia, North Carolina and South Carolina. I was looking to get into UVA or VMI; however, there were no positions in either school at the time.

Sergeant Major Green told me he had two positions open in North Carolina, one at Elizabeth City and one at UNC Charlotte. I didn't know too much about Elizabeth City, but I did know that UNC Charlotte was a larger school and that meant I could train more cadets. I did some research on UNC Charlotte. I liked what I saw and told Sergeant Major I would accept the position.

I cleared Fort Bragg. I was still attached at Walter Reed, but not assigned to the Warrior Transition Brigade there. I was still assigned to Fort Bragg. I went down to Charlotte and became the instructor for the sophomores and also the Operations NCO along with the Ammunition and Training Procurement NCO. I also became the Military History Instructor. I had to go to Fort Leavenworth, Kansas to go through the Military Instructor's History Course.

I was there in Charlotte for a few years, loved the area, good school, but it was time for me to get back to Division, back with the troops. I knew that I couldn't go back to the line because I can't deploy, due to my medical profile. Many of the guys here are faced with the same issue, they are not deployable and they have to realize that. For me, could I fight the system and deploy, perhaps? However, I'm half blind, so if I miss something out there and some soldier pays for it with his life, that's a huge no go for me. I realized that and had to be practical. As an NCO you have to be able to look after your guys, and you can never look after them if you're missing half your vision. Even if you're missing a leg and you're strong everywhere else, and you're out in the field and the leg breaks; now you're a liability instead of an asset.

Anyway, I was looking to get back to the 82nd and I was in contact with SFC Comfort who, at the time, was the Division liaison at Walter Reed and he was a medic. He needed to get on with his career and couldn't stay on there forever. So I asked him if there was some way I could fill his slot when he left. He suggested I get in touch with Division and I said, "Okay, it couldn't hurt to ask."

When I called, I spoke with Sergeant Major Bivens who was the Division Surgeon Sergeant Major. In the meantime, at a conference, I ran into General Cheek who was the former commander of the Warrior Transition Brigade at Walter Reed. He knew who I was because I had been a patient there when he was commander. I had mentioned to him about getting the position at Walter Reed as the Division liaison, and he seemed to be genuinely interested. And so, a number of people helped in getting orders cut for me because I'm in sort of a unique situation.

I'm not up here on TDY (temporary duty), and I'm still assigned to Ft. Bragg. This is a three-year stint for me, being attached here at Bethesda Walter Reed and Ft. Belvoir. Most of the other liaisons are here for a year and then someone else replaces them. It takes a good three months to learn this job, so it's more beneficial to have someone here for three years as opposed to one year. Many of the units are now looking into implementing the scenario that I'm in. So, that's how I ended up here at Bethesda Walter Reed.

My friend's name is Willie, and he's my service dog. I put in for a service dog after a friend of mine, who was an 82nd Captain, had been on the receiving end of some shrapnel in both of his legs. The doctors tried doing limb salvage on both legs for over a year and they saved both legs; however, the nerve damage on his right leg was so bad that he actually requested amputation. After that he had to learn to walk with a prosthetic. He put in for a service dog and received his, and I saw how much that service dog helped him. He got his service dog from Vet Dogs, an organization out of New York City, and they cost quite a bit of money.

So that's where I applied to get Willie. It took about a year until I got him. Normally, they like the person to come up to New York and train along with the dog, but in my case, I was already back in North Carolina. So, they sent a trainer to me for a week and I worked with him and Willie for that week. Willie is half Lab and half Golden Retriever and he was about one and a half years old when I received him. He acts like a buffer on my left side, because I can't see on that side. In crowded environments Willie is there to let people know that my left side is where the problem is so they can give me some room. I can have someone walk up to me from the left, and if they're quiet, I won't know they're there. But with Willie there, it gives me some breathing space.

Willie has been with me now for three years and he accompanies me everywhere I go. He's been on airplanes, elevators, escalators, you name it; Willie's been in it or on it. He's been as far north as New Jersey, as far west as Kentucky and Alabama, and as far south as Florida. He is a good friend to me.

As far as my future plans, some are known and some are unknown. I recently became engaged and that took place on a hot air balloon ride in Georgia with my girlfriend Karen. I had a bottle of Moet champagne on board and I was happy to have her accept my proposal. We are planning a spring wedding in 2013. Karen is a nurse and will be moving up here and we will be here at Bethesda Walter Reed until October of 2014. By that point in time I will have nineteen years in the Army. I'm not so sure it would be good for me to stay on here as liaison because there comes a time when you have to pass the baton. I am on the list for Master Sergeant and when that promotion happens I am required to serve another three years. Because of my unique situation, I have to find jobs that I can fill.

I've thought about heading back to Germany one last time, while I still can. I could be a battlefield observer-controller, a senior battlefield referee. I could always go back to ROTC, but those jobs are hit or miss based on availability. Dealing with cadets is interesting, but dealing with soldiers is much, much more rewarding, because that's what we do. Whereas, cadets are still college students. I'm sure I will find something to suit me, and wherever I go, besides Willie, I will have a new traveling companion.

18

I'D LIKE TO GET OUT
AND PLAY SOME GOLF

M y name is Eric Myers and I am a Staff Sergeant in the
United States Army. Columbus, Ohio is my hometown
and I joined the military in July of 2003. I initially joined for
the college benefits, but came to find out I enjoyed the Army a
little too much, so I stayed in. I received my basic and advanced
training at Fort Sill, Oklahoma. My MOS is 13 Bravo, which is
Field Artillery, and I am a cannon crew member.

After that I went to Fort Benning, Georgia for jump
training. Upon receiving my jump wings, I was assigned to
the 319th Field Artillery at Fort Bragg, North Carolina as part
of 1st Brigade. Then in 2006, I was reassigned to 321st Field
Artillery when 4th Brigade was activated.

My first deployment was in January of 2007, and we
deployed to Paktika Province in Eastern Afghanistan. I spent
fifteen months there and returned back to Fort Bragg. In August
of 2009, I deployed once again, this time for twelve months.
We were deployed to Kandahar in southern Afghanistan. After
completing that mission, we returned to Ft. Bragg.

In February of 2012, I deployed once more to southern
Afghanistan. On 12 May, my squad was sent out to talk to

some villagers just north of our COP (command observation post), just to get some information on what was going on in that area. On our way back in we took some small arms fire. We immediately engaged the enemy, chased them down, and killed one of them. After securing the area, we decided we had done all we could there and headed back towards our COP.

We were in a file formation and I was in the seventh position. In the lead was Sergeant Ford with a mine detector. During the trip back, I stepped on a pressure plate wired to an IED containing about forty pounds of HME. Immediately my ears started ringing and everything went black. I was thrown in the air and everything became slow motion. After I landed, I looked down and noticed both of my legs were gone. I was going in and out of consciousness and only remember bits and pieces, but I do remember the medic, Specialist Steven Rooker, telling me he had the bleeding stopped and I was okay.

The first thing I asked him was, "Is my dick still there?" He assured me that it was and that was all I cared about at that point. I then told him to give me a morphine lollipop, which he did. I thought that it only took ten minutes for the Blackhawk to arrive but was told later that it was more like twenty minutes.

I was the only member of my squad who was injured in the explosion. I remember being carried by the guys on a litter, through a ravine, with chest deep water, and them dropping me on the other side. This caused me excruciating pain, making me scream and yell obscenities at the men. I was having some labored breathing and I remember the medic telling me he was going to give me a needle decompression and that it was going to hurt. I told him, "I don't care; just do it." He did the needle decompression and immediately I could breathe better.

After I was loaded on the chopper, the pain started to set in. I recall looking at my left ring finger and it was hanging on by a piece of skin, so I tried to put it back in place. Of course, it didn't work, and then the medic slapped me in the head and told me to relax. I remember landing at Kandahar but don't remember anything after that until I arrived here at Bethesda Walter Reed. I'm told I spent forty-eight hours there and then I was transferred to Bahgram where I spent three days. They then flew me out to Landstuhl, Germany where I spent another three days before returning stateside to Bethesda Walter Reed.

My right leg is gone above the knee. On my left side, my hip is intact; however, everything below that is gone and I have no femur. I am missing my left ring finger and have extensive damage to my left arm; but I am lucky that no nerves were hit. I also sustained a bad burn on my nose. I do not suffer any TBI (traumatic brain injury). My rehabilitation is coming along fine, and I am on my full prosthetics walking every day.

I have been fortunate to be able to work with the Power Knee, which is a powered knee for above-the-knee amputees that is produced by a company in Iceland. It has a motor inside of it and the knee senses the toe being loaded and swings out for you. It makes it a lot easier to walk with, but it has some downfalls. It's heavier than my other prosthetic, and I had some real issues when I first received it. It will sit a two hundred fifty pound person down and stand him up, but it must be triggered correctly. I've been thrown across the room a couple of times from it because it thought I was trying to stand up and I was really trying to sit down.

My prosthetist is great, and he just returned from Iceland after having the new software updates put in my Power Knee, which he says will help. In fact, I may actually have an opportunity to travel to Iceland this April to check out some of the new stuff they have.

I do not remember who presented me with my Purple Heart. I was put into an induced coma for eight days immediately following the incident, and it was during that time that I received my Purple Heart. I have spent the last ten years at Ft. Bragg; all of my wife's family is from that area. We have made a home there, so I plan on returning there with my wife Laura, and daughter Kinley. I hope to be working at the maintenance facility on Ft. Bragg repairing small arms. That's my goal at this time and I'd also like to get back out on the golf course and play some golf.

I believe in what our military is doing in Afghanistan; however, there are too many Chiefs and not enough Indians. It has become way too political, especially in southern Afghanistan where I have been twice. I've been to the home of the Taliban twice in Kandahar City. The nice guy stuff is not working there as it has in other parts of the country and Iraq. The U.S. soldiers' hands are tied and there are too many rules in the midst of combat for him. He is able to defend himself, but that is about all he can do. With all the military might the United States has, there is a very small amount he can use on this battlefield. One of the reasons is that they are trying to keep civilian casualties to a minimum, and the Taliban exploits this.

I'm proud to have served my country.

19

PERSISTENCE

I am Sergeant First Class Cedric King and I come from Norlina, North Carolina. I joined the military in July of 1995, primarily because I wanted to go to college. I knew that my mom was in no position to help fund a college education for me, and I didn't want to burden her financially for something I was not passionate about. I decided that I needed to go out on my own, and if I made some mistakes, I wanted me to be the one to bear the brunt of it.

I did my basic training at Fort Jackson, and my advanced training at Fort Rucker, Alabama in an aviation specialist program which assists in flight operations. I finished my training there and reported to Fort Bragg, North Carolina in December of 1995. I was assigned to 18th Aviation Brigade initially, and then went to the 82nd Aviation Brigade where I spent three years.

One of the guys in our unit had a ranger tab and I inquired about it. I decided that I needed to earn a ranger tab. I thought, if other guys could do it, there's no reason that I can't. It was one of those things that comes into your head and makes you think. It became an obsession with me. The problem for me was that you couldn't go to ranger school from the MOS that I was in. All the 11 Bravo (infantry) guys were going to ranger school, so I said "Alright, I need to change my MOS." So, I went down to Fort Benning and did a re-class to 11 Bravo. I was already jump qualified due to the fact that when I was assigned to 18th Aviation, I was given the opportunity to go to jump school.

While I was at Fort Benning, they put in a call to ranger branch to see if they could send a few guys over to RIP (ranger indoctrination program). So I'm like, "Yeah, they're putting it right into my hands."

I arrived at the ranger indoctrination program and I passed, so they sent me out to Fort Lewis, Washington, home of the 75th Ranger Regiment. They then sent me to ranger school at Ft. Benning. I was one of the oldest specialists there and I found out it's a lot harder than what I thought. Not so much the physical aspect, but the leadership end of it. I had a hard time with that because, as a leader, you have to infuse the things you know that need to be done into others. And you need to have them want to do it without fear of punishment.

I spent six months in ranger school without passing. That was probably the worst time in my life, but the best thing for me. I didn't know a lot about 11 Bravo stuff, but you spend six months in ranger school and you learn all about infantry related things. To me, it was like the real 11 Bravo school, but what the leaders would learn. I was taught light discipline, patrol basics, land navigation, op orders, you name it. I learned it all. The bad part was that I didn't graduate from ranger school.

I was then shipped back to Ft. Lewis. I got back there and

everybody's like, "Where the hell have you been, King?" At this point in time I have been in the Army for four years, I'm a specialist, and I'm promotable. However, I can't get promoted from the unit I'm in at Ft. Lewis, so I made the decision to go to the 101st Airborne at Ft. Campbell, Kentucky. Also, at this time, I got married, so I've got a lot going on.

I got to Ft. Campbell and found that the pace is a lot slower there. It was okay, but ranger school wasn't on anybody's mind but the top leaders. Who wants to go and be hungry for two or three months, or do without sleep for days at a time? Nobody does. It was still in my mind though. That ranger tab was still burned into my memory. So I started asking around and was told I have to attend pre-ranger school. I said, "What? I just spent six months there."

Anyway, I tell them I want it bad, so they send me back. The first pre-ranger I failed patrols. The second pre-ranger I failed land navigation. The third pre-ranger I passed patrols and land navigation. Now it's November of 2001, and I entered ranger school. I got to the second phase and I broke my foot, and I thought, damn, this is the worst. However, all the time this was teaching me persistence. If there's something you really want to do, you have to stick with it no matter what.

They sent me back to the 101st at Ft. Campbell. During the summer of 2003 I got promoted to E5 Sergeant, and things are starting to settle down after 9/11. The First Sergeant called me in and told me I was going to Iraq. I said, "I can't go to Iraq, I gotta go to ranger school."

I deployed to Iraq with the 1/327th of the 101st Airborne.

We started out in Najaf, and then headed to Mosul. After about six months, out of the blue, they told us they were looking for guys to leave Iraq and go to ranger school. I couldn't believe my luck. Heaven was shining on me. They said they had to have some type of selection process, and I thought, I'll knock that right out of the box.

I destroyed the course and I thought that I got it for sure. Well, they decide to pick this other guy to send. I was disappointed. It so happens, the guy they sent didn't show up for the PT test on time. Ranger school doesn't play that, so the word got back to our unit and I heard about it.

September of 2003 rolled around, and in a month my daughter was going to be born. Now I was thinking that they were gonna send me home. Nope, no ticket home. This was not working out. Soon after, four slots opened up for ranger school, and this time I was slated to go. The beauty of it was that this time I'd get a chance to go home and see my new daughter.

I went to ranger school and failed land navigation. I got recycled into the next class which was in the dead of winter. I was back from the heat of the desert and going to the bitter cold. I must want this pretty bad. It was 2004 and, by the grace of God, I ended up graduating from ranger school. I finally had my ranger tab. For me, all those hard times and lessons taught me about persistence. After that, other schools opened up for me. I attended jumpmaster school, pathfinder school, and air assault, and got assigned as an instructor to jump school. I also worked at pathfinder school for four years.

In July of 2010, I got assigned to the 82nd Airborne Division at Fort Bragg, North Carolina. I felt as if I could be a real asset to the division because of my varied military education up to this point. I became part of the 1/505th PIR. I took over a platoon and in October we went down to Louisiana to JRTC (joint readiness training center). Shortly after we arrived there my First Sergeant got fired. So, we get prep time to prepare and then we go into the box, which is actually simulated war, and then there was the recovery part of it. We were in the box and the Sergeant Major came up to me and told me he needed me to go out there and do the prep time, and plan the patrols and fights. Later on, the Sergeant Major and Colonel came to me and said, "We had to make some changes and you're in the hot seat now."

"What are you talking about? I'm just a platoon sergeant," I said. The Colonel told me he needed me to be his First Sergeant. My whole game plan changed and now I didn't just have my platoon to worry about, I had the entire company to look out for. It actually worked out pretty good. Being a First Sergeant is a tough job but very rewarding.

We came back from JRTC and got orders to deploy to Afghanistan in the summer of 2011. I went there in charge of a company and it was the real thing. All went well for me except that my name didn't come out on the E-8 list for 2011. My Sergeant Major told me the problem was that I didn't have enough time as a platoon sergeant. He said they couldn't give that to me in Iraq because I had already been serving as a First Sergeant. So, I needed to go back to Ft. Bragg and get some time as a platoon sergeant.

I returned to Ft. Bragg and got assigned to 4th Brigade with the 1/508th, who at this time was gearing up to deploy to Kandahar, Afghanistan. I got off a plane at Ft. Bragg in November of 2011 and got back on a plane in February of 2012 to go back to Afghanistan. Now I had a platoon, and the beauty of it was I was already acting as a First Sergeant, so anything that came down was like a piece of cake for me.

They gave me an outpost for my platoon to man, which is called a strong point. It was basically located at an intersection where we stop the traffic going in and out to be checked. Kandahar was one of the worst places because that's where most of the fighters were. In the beginning it was relatively quiet, and then we started hearing shooting from the other platoons in the distance. Then, one day I woke up and heard gunfire in our area and from that day on, for the next five months, it was game on.

We started moving around a lot because you don't stay in one spot for long or the enemy tries to find a weak point and exploit it. You conquer and move, conquer and move. We moved to where the enemy was, attacked it, overtook it, locked it down, and moved on. We hit the hot spots and headed to a place south of brigade headquarters, about six clicks away, called Haji Ramadan. This was an extremely hot spot, located between two very powerful Taliban factions. Their weapon of choice was the IED. They knew that by spreading those around it would limit our maneuverability.

On the morning of July 25th, my platoon was sent out to locate possible IEDs and mainly IED facilities used in the manufacture of the explosives. On this particular patrol, I had the misfortune of stepping on a pressure plate wired to a twenty pound jug of HME. It threw me in the air and everything became slow motion. You don't feel when your legs get cut off. I landed on my back in a crater and then I tried to get up but couldn't. My medic, Specialist Aaron Keller, came over along with a few other guys and they immediately applied tourniquets. I wasn't thinking about what they were doing. I remember thinking that I never wanted to be the kind of leader who would create chaos by my actions. As the platoon sergeant, I was trying to show in the best way I could that everybody needed to remain calm. I had made mental notes, listened to other guys under these circumstances, not to panic. I was still in charge; I was the leader. I just got banged up a little.

I had a young private named Kennedy and he was standing off a bit maintaining security, and I could hear him say to someone, "Man, I can't believe this. It's unbelievable. I never seen anything like this before."

So I said to him, "What? You've never seen anybody get shot before?" Or something like that.

And he said, "No. I can't believe how calm you are."

At that point, that was probably the one thing that really made me feel the best. I never wanted to be the guy who was panicking and screaming. I was extremely proud of the way I handled myself that day.

My platoon RTO got the choppers there in no time and they loaded me onto the Blackhawk while the second bird was flying around pulling security. The chopper took me to Kandahar and they offloaded me and wheeled me into a hospital room. That's the last thing I remember until I woke up here at Bethesda Walter Reed in August. My left leg is gone below the knee and my right leg is gone above the knee. I have prosthetics that I wear and need to get used to. I have no recollection as to who gave me my Purple Heart or where I received it.

Since I've been here the staff and other patients have given me a sense of normalcy because everybody is going through what I'm going through in some way. While you're here, you think, Okay, I can go on; I can do this. The thing about it is that when you go out those gates, nobody understands. They may understand a little and be sympathetic, but they don't participate in the same activities that you do. They don't walk around in wheelchairs. And that has been the toughest part, going out there. When you first get here you think, oh, I hate this place, but then the longer you're here you start to think, hey, maybe this ain't so bad. You realize that you can't stay here forever, that the day's gonna come.

I ended up having one bad day out of all these days I spent in the military. It's been wonderful. I did it all and I had a blast. I wouldn't trade the times I've had in the last seventeen, eighteen years for anything. I had one hell of a good time, and I'd recommend it to other guys out there.

Where do I go from here? Well, I'd like to use this as a springboard for helping and inspiring others. This has been given to me and there's a responsibility to show other people how to overcome these challenges. I'm just one of many who can show people that the impossible can be done. Motivational speaking is on my list, as well as a tri-athlete. Obviously, the lessons learned in the Army have shown me that the persistence I experienced there will carry through for the rest of my life. I refuse to be a quitter.

20

I Was Covered in Sparkles

My name is Matthew Commons. I am a specialist in the United States Army and I am from West Lebanon, Indiana. I joined the Army in 2009 basically to serve my country. I went to Fort Benning, Georgia to complete basic training, infantry school, and jump school. I have been in the military for four years. After completing my training, I was assigned to Fort Bragg, North Carolina as a member of the 82nd Airborne's 1/508th Parachute Infantry Regiment.

My first deployment was from December 2009 until August 2010 to Zabul Province, Afghanistan. The last two months were spent in Kandahar City. The 508th returned to Ft. Bragg and I was there for approximately fifteen months before my next deployment.

My second deployment took place in February 2012, again with the 508th. This time it was to the Zhari District, Kandahar Province, Afghanistan. On the day I was injured my unit was sent to secure a village that was known to have insurgent fighters there. The first part of the mission, upon arrival at the village, was to cordon it off. The next phase was to secure the area by searching for IEDs. We found a few IEDs and then, unfortunately, Specialist Casler stepped on a pressure plate and became the first casualty in our company. He ended up losing his left leg.

Following that incident, 1st platoon kicked into the compound. Following after them was my unit and on the way in there were numerous objects on the ground that had to be checked out before moving forward. We started along this footpath and the first few guys made it to the door of the compound. This was around midnight. I was following my Lieutenant as the radio operator, and as I made my way between a tree and a wall, I stepped on a pressure plate wired to a jug of HME.

I found out later that it was only a partial detonation. I was thrown into the air and landed in a sitting position with my radio pack against the wall. I heard Lieutenant Herbert asking who it was and I told him it was me. I began screaming from the pain. He called for the guys behind us to secure a path to where we were, checking for more IEDs. I looked down and saw both my legs and some blood. I could move my feet but the right foot hurt real bad. The explosion crushed my heel and broke all the bones in my toes. My ankle was also messed up.

The Lieutenant and Staff Sergeant Orozco, my squad leader, were first on the scene, shining their flashlights on me. I was covered in sparkles from the ammonium nitrate, which was part of the IED which didn't detonate. Our medic, Specialist Lucas Oppelt, came over and started working on my foot. He gave me a lollipop and then removed my boot. My right foot was pretty bad, just hanging there. Then they tried to set my right foot. After a while, the medevacs arrived, Blackhawks, and they loaded me onto one of them.

They transported me to Kandahar where I spent a day. While I was there, I received my Purple Heart from General Huggins and Command Sergeant Major Lambert. Then I was off to Bahgram where I spent another day. From there I was flown to Landstuhl, Germany, along with Specialist Casler, the first casualty. He and I made the final trip to Bethesda Walter Reed together on May 27th.

My foot was so badly mangled that I had to have an amputation of my lower right leg. I have been doing physical therapy for the amputation and soon I'll be ready to receive my new prosthetic.

After I conquer the use of my prosthetic, I plan on applying for work with the national park service or for some law enforcement agency.

I am not a big fan of Afghanistan; however, if my country needed me to go again, I would do it.

21

BLOOD WINGS

Author's Note: I first saw Travis Mills on one of my trips to Walter Reed National Medical Center. I was standing at the nurses' station and my liaison told me that there was a soldier in the room across the hall who was an 82nd Airborne trooper who had sustained some rather serious injuries, making him a quadruple amputee. A few days before, the doctors brought him out of a five-day induced coma. Later that day, I returned to the nurses' station for some information when the door to Travis' room opened.

Out came Travis on a motorized wheelchair. He seemed to be confused and was having a very hard time maneuvering it around. I spoke to his wife, Kelsey, explaining why I was there. I told her I knew Travis was in no condition for an interview, but would she would ask him if he was interested in telling me his story. I would be returning in the near future. Then I handed Kelsey my card and left.

On my next visit to Walter Reed National Medical Center two weeks later, I was talking with my liaison when I heard a loud voice, and around the corner came Travis on his motorized wheelchair. It sure hadn't taken him long to conquer the ins and outs of that chariot.

I introduced myself and we spoke briefly. He told me he was extremely busy that day with appointments. I told him it was not a problem and I would be returning again in a few weeks.

During the ride home, I could not get the vision of Travis out of my head, the way he wheeled around the cubicles, smiling and having a good old time. What could I possibly have to complain about after meeting this young man who maintained such a positive attitude in the face of such adversity?

Travis was the kind of guy you immediately gravitate towards. He puts you at ease and, in a room full of people, would no doubt be the center of attention. He was the kind of guy you'd like to sit next to, drink a few beers with, and share a story or two. Staff Sergeant Travis Mills is such a great inspiration for us all, and this is his story.

My name is Travis Mills and my hometown is Vassar, Michigan. I joined the military in March of 2006. Why did I join the military? Things weren't going so well for me at school and I just wanted to get away from it all. So, I signed up for the Army.

I did my basic and advanced training at Fort Benning, Georgia. I remember that after we completed basic, the drill sergeants marched us all downstairs at 2355 hours and had us stand at attention. Then at 2400 hours, they gave the command, "About face! Welcome to AIT, mother fuckers." They hustled us out for some PT and then we went to breakfast. It was a good day to know we were past the first hurdle and moving on.

After finishing AIT, I volunteered for jump training and

stayed at Ft. Benning. I completed my jump training and received my blood wings; that's when your paratrooper wings are hammered into your chest and they draw blood. I was given the option to go to Fort Bragg, home of the 82nd Airborne Division, and I took it. I was excited to see what it was all about.

Initially, I was assigned to the 319th Artillery. Then, 4th Brigade was standing up so I went to the 321st Artillery. I ended up on a personal security detachment for Lt. Colonel Scottie D. Custer, whose great-great uncle was General George Custer who lost his life in the Battle of the Little Big Horn.

I deployed with the 321st Artillery to eastern Afghanistan in January of 2007, to Khost. That deployment lasted fifteen months. While I was there I went out with Lt. Colonel Custer on his trips around the province with the governor, as part of his security team. That's where I met my brother-in-law for the first time, Staff Sergeant Josh Buck. He was a medic on the team. He went home in September to see his child being born and he had some photos of the team. In October his sister got in touch with me, because she thought I was a cutie. R&R was in December for me, so we took a trip to Mexico and it was love at first sight. Shortly after that we were married and it's been four years now. Josh was not happy at all and there was a lot of shit talkin' goin' on. The one time he punched me, which was a weak shot to my shoulder, I told him he wasn't a cowboy. He was from Maine, not Texas.

When I returned to Ft. Bragg after that deployment, I was no longer needed on the security detachment, so I ended up in Alpha Troop, 4-73rd Cavalry Squadron. I deployed with them in 2009 to western Afghanistan near Herat. I returned to Ft. Bragg in 2010.

In February, 2012 I deployed once more with Bravo Troop, 4-73rd Cavalry, to Kandahar, Afghanistan. I was in country about a month and a half and we were going out on a patrol around 1630 hours in the afternoon. I asked my Lieutenant why we were heading out just then. It was almost dinner time, and he just responded, "We need to head on out now, right now."

We arrived at a spot we thought was good and set up the weapons squad. The 1st and 2nd squads headed towards the town, while 3rd and 4th squads set up. I was 4th squad leader and we had set up the guns, the M240 machine guns. My ammo bearer found a spot he thought was good to set up at. I approved it and told him to get the gunner up to the site. I set my bag full of ammo down right on top of a pressure plate. When I came to I noticed my right arm was gone, my right leg was gone, and my left leg was just hanging on. Then, on my left hand I still had my thumb, and index finger; the rest of it was a mess. I remember reaching up my hand and yelling to my Lieutenant that we were going to need some help over here.

The medic, Sergeant Daniel Bateson, came running over after he recovered from being knocked out from the blast. I began yelling at him to get away from me, to just let me go, and tend to the other guys who got hit. He told me, "With all due respect Sergeant Mills, shut the fuck up and let me do my job."

I was flipping out, yelling for my team leader, Specialist Ryan Berrio, aka The Riot. My ammo bearer, Brandon Fessey, had been going up and down the mound with a mine detector, and little did he know, it wasn't working. I was behind him and I could hear the mine detector making noises. Turns out, there were 13 IEDs in the area we set up in.

I was still yelling and asking how the rest of my guys were and someone yelled, "They're gonna be okay," and that calmed me down a bit. I was laying there and Doc was checking me over, and I started making jokes about my manhood, "It's a grower, not a shower. Quit looking at it and making fun of it, Doc."

Doc gave me a fentanyl lollipop. You're supposed to suck on it, but I bit into it and chewed it up. I said, "Hey Doc, give me another one."

He said he couldn't, but the only time I was in real pain was when they stuck an IV right into my sternum to replace fluids I had lost. Doc made sure all four tourniquets were in place but I had a severed artery under my right armpit and I was losing blood. They were successful at closing off the artery, and shortly after that the Blackhawk arrived.

They loaded me onto the bird and then someone else was yelling like they were in pain. It turned out to be Riot who had been injured around the upper part of his leg. I yelled to the flight medic but he couldn't hear me, so I motioned for him to remove his helmet. I told him to make sure my guys had water and to assure them they'd be okay. Then I yelled over to Riot to calm down; he needed to stop yelling out. Fessey, who had been twenty feet away, took shrapnel to his face, and luckily his glasses saved his eyes. I was told later that the explosive was a jug of HME, which is common.

During the flight, the medics were giving us water and they were pretty excited about the whole incident. They wrote a letter to me later on saying how brave I was, looking out for my men even though I had sustained such major injuries. But, my men were what mattered to me in the long run.

Anyway, we landed at Kandahar and they put me in the ambulance, and I was talking to them the whole time. They got me to the operating table and started lifting my left leg and I kept telling them to leave it alone. That's when the Doc said "okay," and they sedated me and I went out. I was told that when they removed what was left of my pants, my left leg came off with them. At that point in time, I became a triple amputee.

When my brother-in-law, Josh, found out what had happened, he punched a wall and broke his hand. They told him I was probably going to die. Ironically, they sent him to Kandahar, where I was, to get treated. He hooked up with me there and told them he wanted to accompany me on the flight to Bahgram. They tried to stop him but, he said, "I'm fuckin' goin' anyway." At Bahgram, on 12 April, they cut off what remained of my mangled left hand, making me a quadruple amputee. Josh then flew with me to Landstuhl, Germany.

On 14 April, they decided to wake me up. Why? Supposedly Abraham Lincoln was assassinated on that day, and also the Titanic sank. And, on top of that, it just might have been my twenty-fifth birthday. Yeah, they woke me up for that; can you believe it? My brother-in-law was sitting next to me and the first thing I asked him was, "How are my soldiers?"

He told me Riot was there in Germany with me, and he was

doing fine and was up and walking around. He told me Fessey was in Kandahar and was also doing well. I underwent four surgeries there to repair and cleanse my wounds.

I asked Josh if I was paralyzed and he said, "No."

I said, "Josh, you don't have to lie to me; I can't move my fingers and toes."

He said, "Travis man, I'm sorry, you don't have them anymore."

He told me the story about what had happened and I said, "Oh, okay." Then I went back to sleep. After that, everything was kind of a blur, because my pain got to be so bad, ten out of ten, that they had to put me into a Ketamine coma for five days.

That was crazy. When I came out of it later on, I couldn't remember a lot of what had happened. I'd remember being in a car chase, up a tree, being part of whatever was on television, like being part of the Seinfeld show. I also wasn't talking to my parents and my wife. They'd come into my room and I would just look away, not listen to them or talk to them. The reason was, I was embarrassed because my guys got hit and the enemy getting me really sucked. However, there's really no quit or defeat in me, mainly because of my beautiful daughter, Chloe. So I say, "Fuck those pussies, they fight like bitches. They might have blown me up, but they didn't take anything from me."

I arrived here at Bethesda Walter Reed on 17 April, and my brother-in-law came with me. I have been doing well since arriving here. My left hand is myoelectric, so it opens and closes reacting to the movement of the muscles in my forearm. My outpatient therapist has helped me to learn basically everything

I need to know for everyday life. The best part is that I can shower by myself, make a sandwich and feed myself. My right arm and hand are not so technologically advanced but, down the road, who knows? Everything I do is a whole new learning experience. I also have these short legs I can attach and I'm down closer to my daughter's level to play with her. It's really neat. I have one amputation above the knee and one below the knee. I have my prosthetic power legs that work quite well also.

My Purple Heart was pinned on me while I was on the table in Kandahar and then my brother-in-law held onto it for me. While I was here at Bethesda Walter Reed, the Purple Heart Foundation came in and presented me with one. There was supposed to be a formal presentation at Ft. Bragg after a run the one morning with the other guys who got hit, but somehow it got screwed up. I've been recognized enough. I know what I did, and it wasn't made to be about me. I know I'm one of five quadruple amputees from the war, and I just try to do what I can. I go over to the fourth floor nurses' station and find out who's new and talk to them and say, "Look, it doesn't get much worse than this. I'm just here to let you know that it will get better."

Now, I run into guys who I went to see months ago and they're like, "Wow, man, you were such an inspiration for me, thanks."

As far as any future plans, I want to get out of here as soon as possible so my daughter doesn't have to grow up in a hospital. I plan on returning to North Carolina and making a home for my family and having a backyard with a swing set for Chloe to enjoy. I, and my brother Zack, would like to open a non-profit organization to help the families of wounded service men and women who come here so they don't have to quit their jobs to be here. I'm also playing around with the idea of being a motivational speaker.

My afterthoughts about the war are simple. I'm a soldier and I train with the guy on my right and the guy on my left. My country sends me wherever, and I go and do my job. As far as Afghanistan goes, I wasn't there for the people, or what they need; I could care less. I wasn't there for the Afghan people; I was there for my soldiers. I don't get wrapped up in all that political stuff. It's not for me to say "yes or no." It's up to me to do my duty. If the United States needs me there, then I go. I'd go back again if I could. Sign me up.

AFTERWORD

Freedom is not free; it comes at a very high price. Just take the tour of Arlington National Cemetery, Indiantown Gap National Cemetery, or any other cemetery in whose hallowed ground our nation's fallen heroes lie. They died for our freedom.

When you live in a free country like the United States, you never know what it feels like to thirst for freedom. I know I don't. Have you ever thirsted for water? I imagine it would be something similar. Remember this: "Greater love hath no man than this, that a man lay down his life for his friends." Ask any of the men and women in this book, or any other wounded warrior. I am sure they can tell you the price of freedom: an arm, a leg, fingers, eyesight, nightmares, brains rattled by concussion. No matter the cost, they paid the price for freedom.

In the many interviews I did for this book, I found it interesting that not a single wounded warrior had any hatred or remorse because of his or her injuries. Each one has learned to work with the cards that were dealt to them. They all have future goals and ambitions; some will remain in the military and some will get out and move on to a different calling.

I am very fortunate to have met such wonderful human beings, and I am eternally grateful that I was able to spend time with them. They have truly inspired me, and I know they will be an inspiration to many others who will cross paths with them.

"God bless them all; the long and the short and the tall."

PHOTOGRAPHS

Top left: Jonathan Tompkins;
Top right: Idi Mallari;
Above: Kelly Oldfather;
Left: Leon Brimm (R).

Above left: Jared Lemon; *Above right:* Joe Yantz;
Below left: Tim Senkowski; *Below right:* Alex Jauregui.

Above left: May Agurto; *Above right:* Dave Smith;
Below left: Patrick Percefull; *Below right:* Wyatt Harris.

Top left: Christian Brown;
Top right: Ken Swartz;
Above: John Carnes;
Right: Jonathan Grundy.

Above left: Eric Myers; *Above right:* Cedric King;
Below left: Matt Commons; *Below right:* Travis Mills.

Author Joseph Baddick with LtCol Oliver L. North, USMC (Ret.)

About the Author

Joseph Baddick served as an 82nd Airborne Division paratrooper before working for the Pennsylvania Department of Corrections for twenty years. Originally from the coal region, he now resides with his wife Sheila in Berks County, PA. When Joe is not working for the Miller-Keystone Blood Center, he enjoys golf, winemaking, fine dining, traveling, the outdoors, and spending time with his grandchildren. His first book, *My Hero, My Son*, tells the story of his son A.J., an 82nd Airbone Division paratrooper who died in Iraq.

If you would like to contact Joe, please feel free to do so by sending an email to the following address:

JosephBaddick@gmail.com

CPSIA information can be obtained at www.ICGtesting.com
Printed in the USA
BVOW082345290513

321964BV00004B/9/P